Edward Hopper

One Wife too Many

Edward Hopper

One Wife too Many

ISBN/EAN: 9783744659215

Printed in Europe, USA, Canada, Australia, Japan

Cover: Foto ©Thomas Meinert / pixelio.de

More available books at **www.hansebooks.com**

ONE WIFE TOO MANY;

OR,

RIP VAN BIGHAM.

A TALE OF TAPPAN ZEE.

BY

EDWARD HOPPER.

NEW YORK:
PUBLISHED BY HURD AND HOUGHTON,
459 Broome Street.
1867.

CONTENTS.

———

ONE WIFE TOO MANY.

—◆—

I.

TAPPAN ZEE.

IN the olden days when Jonathan
   Was but an unweaned, feeble child
   And his inheritance a wild,
Snatched at by every robber clan ;

His guardian angel flew abroad,
   To distant lands and isles afar,
   With banner of a guiding star,
And golden trumpet sounding loud ;

And called the people to his aid,
   To keep his life inviolate ;
   And that for his divine estate
The sure foundations might be laid.

Though Heaven assisted at his birth,
   And gave him as his heritage,

To hold, when he should come of age,
Vast realms of his good mother Earth,

He needed help of hearts and hands,
  Brave-hearted men, the strong and true,
  To do what brave good men could do,
To fell his woods, and clear his lands,

And lay foundations deep and strong,
  And build his palace worthily,
  With wings to stretch from sea to sea,
And roof of stars to last as long

As heaven's own star-lit canopy
  O'erspreads the ever-sounding sea ;
  As long as winds and waves are free,
And long as man loves liberty.

None but the bold, none but the free,
  Not many pampered rich, or great,
  Were called to rear his glorious state,
But men made strong by poverty ;

Men seasoned by the fire and flood ;
  Men bruised by tyrants' threshing flails,
  And winnowed by the winnowing gales,
Like wheat from chaff, — the sound and good.

A holy shrine's pure worshipers,
　　From shivered tree-roofs' sacred spots, —
　　The Puritans, the Huguenots,
And glorious, free-born Hollanders:

These saw the angel from afar, —
　　The guardian of our infant land,
　　With golden trumpet in his hand;
And followed his far-reaching star.

O'er ocean's stormy depths they came,
　　Led by the Angel clothed in fire,
　　With souls which faith and hope inspire,
And love, with its celestial flame.

The Puritan sought the rock-bound coast,
　　To match his own stern character;
　　The Huguenot and Hollander
A sunnier heart and home would boast.

A fitting home our heroes found
　　By Tappan Zee, whose waters fell
　　From some celestial spring, or well,
In which the smiles of heaven abound.

For all the smiles of heaven we trace
　　In its clear depths; the sunbeams bright
　　By day, and gentle stars by night,
Shine constant in its lovely face.

The guide to whom the boon was given
   To show to men's admiring eyes
   The river strayed from Paradise,
When man was from the garden driven,

The silvery Half-Moon's car bestrode,
   And gave the white-winged steeds the reins;
   Then, with a hero's pluck and pains,
Across the globe, in search he rode;

Nor reined his steeds until he came
   Upon the glorious river-tide
   Which men, in gratitude and pride,
Have ever since called by his name.

'T was meet that Hudson's countrymen,
   For whom Heaven had a special choice,
   In such a pilot should rejoice,
And pitch their tents where his had been.

'T was thus our fathers, good and wise,
   The path of empire Westward traced,
   And thus their worthy feet were placed
Within the New World's Paradise.

With these came Dirk Van Bigham's son,
   Heroic Rip, too early torn
   From his young bride, to trouble born,
Ere their twin-life had scarce begun.

II.

THE MARRIAGE.

Oh merrily, merrily ring the bells,
In Amsterdam, the marriage-bells ;
And every voice with joy foretells,
　Nothing distrustful, nothing loth,
　Joy for the bride and bridegroom both.

Merry and clear and laughing the bells ;
Fairies have entered their brazen cells,
　To rattle the steeple down ;
And every one says, from street to street,
The bridegroom is gentle, the bride is sweet,
　And a better match you could not meet
　In any Netherland town.

The joy leaps down from every face,
And trips along from place to place,
　And rattles from every tongue,
As if the heads of all the people
Were each a belfry of a steeple,
　In which a bell was rung.

And bells pour blessings from every sound,
As the sun pours sunbeams on the ground,
　On bride and bridegroom young ;

And no one asks, nor wonders whether
The two young hearts they 've chimed together
  Shall wish they 'd ne'er been rung.

Oh merrily, merrily ring the bells,
Merrily ring the marriage-bells,
And every one with joy foretells,
  ` Nothing distrustful, nothing loth,
    Joy for the bride and bridegroom both.

Their hearts were married long before,
  And now the formal troth and plight
And sacred seal could add no more
  Than outward symbols of the right
By which they held each other fast,
Through good and ill, while life should last.
From early childhood they had known
  And loved each other, till at length,
Their hearts, which had together grown,
  Were one in their maturer strength,
  And one, in solemn form to-day,
  Only that they might weep at parting;
For Rip must leave her on the morrow.
  On cheeks of love the tears were starting
That dimmed their bridal day with sorrow;
For he must sail, on venture bold,
With spirit of his fathers old,
To seek for her both lands and gold.

This was the plan agreed upon,
And this the cloud upon their sun.
Katrina feared for fearless Rip —
What evils might befall the ship!
What lurking storms on every hand,
What dangers in the distant land,
That new and untried world, where he
Would build their home beyond the sea ?
This was the cloud upon her brow;
This made his bride so lovely now, —
More lovely that her eyes were dim
Because her tears were shed for him;
More precious to his loving heart
As treasure is from which we part.

He would not have her weaker form
Go brave the hardship and the storm
Till first he built his bird a nest
In the bright regions of the West,
Then she might fly and be at rest.

And she, though brave as bride may be,
Had inward tremblings at the sea,
From that mysterious, inborn dread
With which her soul at birth was wed;
Or from wild legends she had read; —
How their forefathers stained the flood
With deeds of glory and of blood,
And cleft with angry swords the waves
Both for their own and foemen's graves.

III.

THE LEGEND.

THEIR ancestors were vikings old,
  Brave rovers of the sea ;
And, in the bloody battles, bold
  As boldest men could be.

They fought the Turk and broke his power,
  When at the height was he ;
And saw his flaming crescent lower
  Upon the crimson sea.

Nor this was all ; — alack the day !
  They turned and fought each other,
When Christian raised his hand to slay
  And rob his Christian brother.

But these sad years went trembling by ;
  And lo ! a peaceful dove,
With holy message from the sky,
  Had changed their hate to love.

And Rip Van Bigham and his bride —
  The good Katrine Barthold,
Had grown together, side by side,
  In love, from foemen old.

But sweet Katrine much feared the sea,
   And shuddered at the waves,
Which their bold foemen ancestry
   Had made each others' graves.

For she had heard the legend old
   Of one whose name she bore,
The cruel viking, Bad Barthold,
   Who died long years before.

A bloody death he died at last
   And perished on the land,
At Groningen, where life flowed fast,
   From War's avenging hand.

For many and many a foe had he,
   When victor in the strife,
Cast headlong in the foamy sea,
   Though pleading for his life.

Among them was an only son,
   A widow was his mother ;
He was her staff to lean upon ;
   On earth she had no other.

With her he had a youthful wife,
   And little one beside ;
For these he pleaded for his life, —
   His mother, babe, and bride.

" I am my mother's only son !
   She has on earth no other ;
I have a wife and little one !
   My mother, Oh my mother ! "

In vain he pleads ; in vain he kneels ;
   For wives, or babes, or mothers,
Barthold the Bad no mercy feels,
   But slays him with the others.

Oh yes ! in spite of cries like these,
   While yet his lips are speaking,
He hurls him to the boiling seas,
   Amid the groans and shrieking.

He does not sink, as others do,
   But swims and follows after ;
Now wailing forth his plea of woe,
   And now his maniac laughter.

" I have a wife and little one ;
   Oh save us for each other !
I am a widow's only son :
   My mother, Oh my mother ! "

The day grew calm, the work was done,
   And hushed the wild commotion ;
And many a corpse sank, with the sun,
   Beneath the blood-stained ocean.

But still this victim would not die,
　　But followed in his wake,
And prayed, with that same pleading eye,
　　For that same mercy's sake.

The viking trembled in his bed,
　　He trembled ever after ;
He tried to think his victim dead,
　　But heard his groans and laughter.

He saw him at his vessel's side,
　　Swimming as heretofore,
Where'er he sailed on oceans wide,
　　To what far-distant shore.

When all was calm, or mid the storm,
　　By day and in the night,
He saw that youthful hero's form,
　　And trembled at the sight.

Saw his despairing, pleading eye
　　Beseeching for his life ;
And heard his plaintive, broken cry
　　For mother, babe, and wife.

He left the sea with bags of gold,
　　And all a viking's glory, —

2

Barthold the Brave, the bad Barthold;
　　Then told his fearful story.

But still the scene would follow him
　　From shore to distant shore,
And still he saw his victim swim
　　And plead as heretofore.

And when he met, at Groningen,
　　His bloody end, in battle,
His victim's prayer was heard by men
　　In Barthold's last death-rattle, —

" I have a wife and little one;
　　Oh save us for each other!
I am my mother's only son:
　　My mother, Oh my mother!"

IV.

PROGNOSTICATIONS.

KATRINA's good uncle, old Wolfert Van Gruntz,
Had an eye for the dark, and saw it at once,
And flew about in it with the ease of a bat,
And revelled therein with the gust of a rat.
He thought Rip's adventure was wild and all that,
Not worth the clay pipe in the band of his hat;

And such a wild-goose chase filled him with dread,
For he saw the shadows of dangers, he said,
The storms in mid-ocean ; the breakers ahead ;
Sharks following the ship, to eat him when dead ;
And if he was wrecked and arrived, on a spar,
Without money, or clothes, what could he do there
But lie down and die, without saying a prayer.
Besides, the wild Indians had talons like hawks,
And lurked in the forests and bushes and stalks,
All hungry and ready, by night and by day,
To swoop like hawks, and to pounce on their prey.
Those savages, red with the stain of men's blood,
Had been swept to that land by tempest and flood.
By the wrath of Almighty, chasing them fast,
Till they got to that unpeopled world at last,
With the red mark of Cain on every brow,
And murder at heart, and they had it there now ;
And a man at a meal was a very small thing
For one of those red human hawks on the wing.

To which Rip replied, that Uncle Van Gruntz
Was always predicting his pigs would be runts ;
And of all his fine calves he had n't a calf
Worth the milk that it took from the cow, by half ;
If he set an old hen the eggs would n't hatch,
Or if they did, then the chickens would scratch
And tear up his garden and tulips, perhaps ;
And to close up accounts would die of the gapes.

If it rains he says it will drown all the crops,
And predicts a long drought as soon as it stops;
Last year he foretold a great famine and dearth,
That would starve all mankind and ruin the earth,
Because of the drought; and when that was over,
And the earth fairly groaned with the grain and
    clover,
Then he said that such crops did far greater harm
Than famine, because they exhausted the farm.
Our good Uncle Gruntz must grumble, or die:
He once tried to sing, but his song was a sigh.
On the brightest of days Uncle Gruntz sees a
    cloud
In shape of a coffin, a hearse, or a shroud;
He seems to take pleasure in being in trouble,
And gets all he can of it, then makes it double.
When a boy he used to play at soap-bubble,
As all children do; but he had the knack
Of making the brightest of bubbles look black;
And all the bright hopes that cheer other men
With Uncle Van Gruntz are those bubbles again.
To *look at all things as they are*, is his pride;
Then turns them all over to find their dark side;
And casts his black horoscope farthest ahead
To find for his pleasure what most people dread.
And even the sun is dark to Van Gruntz, —
He *knows* it is so, for he looked at it once.

To which Van Gruntz made cautious answer
    mild,
For sweet Katrina's sake, his sister's child,
And for young Rip, because he loved him well,
And feared for both what he must needs foretell.
" You know how Mount Pilatus raves with storm,
And has so raved since Pontius Pilate's form,
Ages ago, was found upon its peak.
All travellers tell us that the wail and shriek,
Like that of human soul in blank despair,
Are always heard in its most dismal air, —
The wails and shrieks of him who perished there.
For he, the bad judge of the Crucified,
Had wandered to that mountain-top, and died.
Accursed, through earth he wandered, seeking
    rest,
And finding none, till on that lonely crest
He raved his soul out; and the shuddering Mount
Took up his wailings; — such is the account.
And from that time, like Pilate's troubled breast,
The desolate Mount Pilatus cannot rest;
No living thing, that has the touch of pain,
Amid its furious tempests can remain:
No bird ere tries its song : no foot, nor wing,
Can stand its ceaseless storms, — no living thing, —
Where Pilate's curse has left its deathless sting,
And where his groans, that to the mountain cling,
From rock to rock their ceaseless echoes fling.

" And like Pilatus hath the ocean been
Since our forefathers stained it with their sin.
Our fathers, in the bloody days of old,
As fierce in battle as their hearts were bold,
Bequeathed their wrath to storm-fiends of the seas,
To 'venge their deaths, by cruel enemies,
On children's children down to coming ages:
These lash the ocean till it foams and rages,
While phantom ships and angry spirits sweep,
As with a besom, the tumultuous deep.
For blood-stained ghosts, at sea, can never rest,
But course the ocean in their vengeful quest,
Flying on clouds and winds, from crest to crest;
And with the voice of storms for vengeance cry
To angry Heaven that thunders its reply.
Thus armed with wrath each wide-mouthed, hun-
     gry wave
Opens its jaws to be a human grave.
'T is thus our treasure, thus our kith and kin
Must pay the debt of our forefathers' sin ;
For much remains unpaid, though poverty
By wreck and loss, has cursed our family."

To whom the good Katrina made reply : —
" Lay not our losses to the angry sky,
Nor to the hate of ancient enemies
Seeking revenge upon the angry seas.
Our new religion tells us, ' God is love ; '

And He hath sent again the gentle Dove,
That calmed the troubled deep at the beginning,
To turn men's souls from hate and angry sinning.
Kind Heaven forgives; and they who hope for
   heaven
Forgive as they do hope to be forgiven.
The wrath of men cannot forever last;
Our fathers' feuds are buried with the past;
And Rip and I are married just to prove
That our forefathers' hate has turned to love."

 But still she owned a dread, a strange commo-
   tion,
She knew not why, at sight or sound of ocean : —
Its gentlest tones seemed to her ears, she said,
Like everlasting moanings of the dead;
Its sight was symbol of the desolate,
The lone and drear, — the lost from hope's estate,
And this strange dread was heightened, she con-
   fessed,
By the sad words Van Gruntz had just addressed,
And stood like nightmare on a sleeper's breast :
She tried to throw it off, but vainly tried;
And mid the shadows of that eventide
Thus sang for Rip, his good and loving bride :

KATRINA'S SONG.

WHEN bright young Hope comes tempting us
    To try an unknown shore,
She tells us of the halcyon days
    Laid up for us in store ;
But tells us not what starless nights
    And dangers lie before.

The glorious land that shines afar,
    Beyond the distant sea,
On Nature's breast, without a jar,
    Asleep so peacefully,
Seems like a far-off distant star,
    An unknown world to me.

And you seem taking wings to fly,
    My love, to that far shore;
You seem like one about to die,
    Whom I shall see no more,
Whose soul is starting for the sky,
    For treasure laid in store.

I know 't is foolish so to speak,
    Nor is this fancy true ;
I know and feel that I am weak,
    And cannot say adieu ;

For all the world looks blank and bleak,
  Since I must part from you.

With all my treasure on the deep, —
  My husband dear, my own,
Launched forth to tempt the storms that sweep
  The broad Atlantic down, ·
I cannot help it, I must weep,
  Though Heaven may smile, or frown.

To whom brave Rip, rejoicing in his bride,
Repressing much, right hopefully replied :

RIP'S SONG.

BLESSINGS forever on my wife !
  Come, let me dry your tears ;
Be cheerful, sweet Katrine, my life !
  And throw away your fears,
For we are warriors in a strife
  Which Heaven approves and cheers.

We part but for a year or two,
  And then, my gentle bride
Shall see what kindly Hope can do
  To help us stem the tide ;
In this Old World are cares and woe,
  But joy the other side.

The heart grows strong by hope, my love ;
　　I see the land draw near,
The storm-clad billows all remove,
　　And dangers disappear ;
And while your prayers ascend above
　　I cannot feel a fear.

When I am gone, Katrine, I know
　　You will be strong and brave ;
You will not think of grief and woe,
　　Of wreck and watery grave,
And gloomy caverns far below
　　The ocean's stormy wave.

But think how happy I am there,
　　In that far-distant land,
Where the golden sun and God's free air
　　Uphold the toiler's hand,
And Freedom makes all things look fair
　　With her bewitching wand.

And think how few shall be the days
　　Ere we shall meet again,
In that bright world whose golden rays,
　　Wed with the silvery rain,
Set all the harvest fields ablaze
　　With sheaves of golden grain.

When there we meet, our griefs and fears
    Shall drown in joy's sweet stream ;
And all our parting pangs and tears
    But trifles then will seem ;
And our long-absent months or years,
    A short forgotten dream.

There with a home, in some bright spot,
    How happy we shall be ;
With busy toil to cheer our lot,
    And honest industry ;
The richest monarch then will not
    Be happier than we.

And you will pray when I am gone, —
    Prayer is your carrier-dove, —
And so when you are left alone
    You 'll send it oft above,
With message to our Father's throne ;
    And He will bless our love.

And thus together we shall meet,
    Though parted by the sea, —
We 'll bow before His mercy-seat,
    And there together be ;
For I will pray for you, my sweet,
    And you will pray for me.

And God will watch o'er me and you,
　　And lead us by the hand ;
And keep us safe, and good, and true,
　　Till we together stand,
Clasped in each others' arms anew,
　　In that far-distant land.

Now you are stronger, Kate, for this
　　Is not our funeral knell ;
Though no one knows how hard it is,
　　Nor human tongue can tell,
For us to give the parting kiss,
　　And speak the word, Farewell !

V.

THE VOYAGE.

THE tide was up ; and so were Van Dam's sails ;
He gave the word, and bounding seaward went
The *Rollicker*, while prayers for prosperous gales
Arose ; but some saw signs of ill portent.
She sailed on Friday, and Van Gruntz well knew
That nothing good could ever come of that ;
No matter how propitious breezes blew,
A storm would soon turn up and knock her flat.
Perchance might drive her back ; he hoped it
　　would ;

For then the venturous Rip would believe his
    word ;
And stay at home, as every bridegroom should,
To warm the nest of his new-mated bird.
He knew 't would blow great guns ; and very
    soon ;
For when the dykes all trembled, and the forms
Of horses in the clouds dashed on the moon,
They never failed to bring tremendous storms !
Katrine, whose heart was hung 'twixt hope and
    fear,
Soon felt the influence of Van Gruntz's signs ;
And thus invited many a needless tear,
And sorrow's ploughshare with its furrowing lines.
Full many a day and night she watched the
    clouds,
And saw wild horses dashing at the moon,
Then, wheeling seaward, charge, in snorting
    crowds,
And sweep the ocean !   Such Van Gruntz's boon
To one he loved, nor for the world would harm ;
His spirit cast a shadow on her heart,
And his ill omens filled her with alarm,
Till every rising wind would make her start.
With all her treasure freighted in one ship,
And 'gainst that ship the storm-fiends' fearful hate
Gathering the tempest-bolts to let them slip, —
No wonder that she trembled for its fate !

And when the news came in of the great storm
Which few weeks later vexed the giant sea,
And left full many a ship a helpless form,
Her fears became a sickening agony.
Two ships had sailed that day in company,
But one engrossed her thoughts by night and day;
That one had periled many in the sea,
But of these many *one* was chief alway.
" What fate is his ? where is my husband now ?
Has he outlived the storm ? — or do the waves
Press down their mountain weight upon his brow,
Where thousands sleep in ocean's gloomy caves ? "
Hope came to lift the darkness, with his lamp —
A feeble lamp in such a fearful night ;
But still he softly smoothed her pillow damp,
And cheered her aching bosom with its light ;
Then gently rocked her weary heart to sleep ;
And drove away her fears and cares at once ;
Till sudden nightmare, monster of the deep,
Aroused her, in the shape of old **Van Gruntz.**

THE STORM.

THE ship is on the sea ;
   The storm is in the sky ;
The maddened winds are free ;
   The angry waves dash high.

Loosed from their dens in the deep
   Storm-fiends howl in the shrouds,
And fierce red lightnings leap
   Like demons from the clouds.

Manhood and strength, in vain,
   Buffet the tempest's power ;
The ship darts on the main,
   Nearer her doom each hour.

Beauty and childhood stand
   Pale on the trembling deck :
O God ! stretch forth Thine hand,
   The raging billows check !

" Stand to your posts, ye brave !
   You never flinched of old ;
Life, or a watery grave :
   Hark ! death is in the hold !

" Strive ye for woman's sake ;
   Strive for the infant's tear ;
Your bold hearts cannot quake ;
   The sailor knows no fear ! "

Shrill was that manly cry
   Unto those gallant men ;
The tear was in their eye,
   And fierce the struggle then.

But fiercer grows the gale,
　　And louder than before,
Till every tattered sail
　　And shivered mast gives o'er.

The frightened infant clings
　　Fast to its mother's breast;
And strange! the weird wind sings
　　The little one to rest!

For prayers have gone to Heaven,
　　And lo! an angel form,
With rainbow-crown, is given
　　To still the angry storm.

Full many have found a grave,
　　And billowy winding-sheet,
Where oft the mournful wave
　　Their requiem shall repeat.

Low is their pearly bed,
　　Beneath the Atlantic deep,
Where winds, that wail the dead,
　　Can never wake their sleep.

But where that angel-form
　　The crown of rainbow wears
No victims has the storm,
　　For God has heard their prayers.

It stands by the old *Goed Vrouw*,
   Which sailed with the *Rollicker;*
God guide her consort now
   To come and rescue her!

THE RESCUE.

THE *Rollicker* had met the blast,
   And laughed the fiends to scorn ;
But now was scudding with bare mast,
   With sails and rigging torn.

For maniac winds, from storm-burst clouds,
   Came flying down in wrath,
And strained her timbers, rent her shrouds,
   And drove her from her path.

And wide-mouthed waves with foamy lip,
   All hungry for a meal,
Pursued and struck the flying ship
   With blows that made her reel.

But still the captain smoked his pipe,
   For he was cool and calm,
And held the helm with sturdy gripe,
   Did jolly Rip Van Dam.

3

Rotund of body, stout of soul,
　　And strong of will, of course,
He had the ship at his control,
　　As rider has a horse.

He bade her fly before the wind,
　　Across the yeasty flood,
Like horse that leaves the wolves behind
　　That chase him for his blood.

He smoked his pipe and told his crew
　　That winds were made to blow;
And what his brave good ship could do
　　They knew, or ought to know.

" Aye, aye, sir; Captain, that we ought ! "
　　And all the crew were calm;
So well the spirit brave they caught
　　Of doughty Rip Van Dam.

And well the ship obeyed his will,
　　And strained her for the flight;
Till tired winds and waves were still,
　　And wolves were out of sight.

But many a weary league it cost, —
　　That flight by night and day;
And many feared the ship was lost,
　　So long was her delay.

To steer men right, yourself be right ;
    To make men brave, be brave ;
For truth and right are the beacon light,
    On land and on the wave.

With such good chart did Rip Van Dam
    Take the helm of ship and crew ;
And steered them safe when seas were calm,
    And through the tempest too.

With such good chart the *Rollicker*
    Soon found the wrecked *Goed Vrouw*,
And won the name of *Rescuer*,
    To crown her storm-scarred brow.

The crew with cheers received the name,
    But spake as sailors can, —
That any man would do the same
    If he were half a man.

The captain smoked his pipe with joy,
    Though striving to look calm,
And talked and laughed like any boy,
    Did jolly Rip Van Dam.

And smiling skies and many a prayer,
    That blessings ever brings
Came down to bless the *Rollicker*,
    And angels lent her wings.

So straight she flew to the New World,
　By men and angels blest,
Where safely moored, her sails all furled,
　She glory found, and rest.

VI.

MANHATTA.

MANHATTA, daughter of the Manitou,
　From whom she came, in primal days,
With rustic crown of beauty on her brow,
　Is worthy still the lyric praise.

Kissed by the zephyrs of the land and sea,
　Embraced by twin-encircling arms
Of river nymphs, in loving rivalry,
　She stood unrivalled in her charms.

Bright skies looked down and smiled into her face ;
　And she for blushing honors given,
Raised her crowned head, with modesty and grace,
　And breathed her fragrant thanks to heaven.

Up through her narrow pathway, from the sea,
　All nations flock, with sails unfurled ;
And in her bounteous lap, admiringly,
　They cast the tribute of the world.

Her gates hospitable are open wide,
    With ample cheer for every one;
And guests keep pouring in, with every tide,
    From rising to the setting sun.

Downtrodden nations, flying from their chains,
    The sons of sorrow from abroad;
Children of poverty and toil and pains,
    That from earth's tyrants cry to God: —

All kindreds, peoples, — every tribe and tongue
    Come flocking to her opened gates,
Which constant, day and night, are open flung;
    And she, with smiles, their coming waits.

The poor feast on her wealth; the halt and lame
    Stand up erect, and walk like men;
The blind eyes see; and, warmed by her free
      flame,
    The dead revive and live again.

All languages are spoken in her streets;
    The exile from his fatherland
A brother in the passing stranger meets,
    Who speaks his name and takes his hand.

The Homestead of the world! here all mankind
    May build their hearths, and light their fire;

And rear the sacred altars to their mind,
   As faith and holy love inspire.

Her citizens go forth through all the earth,
   With crown of manhood on their brow,
Proud of the glorious city of their birth, —
   The child of the great Manitou.

Manhatta tempted Rip to take repose
   And lodgings in her fairy isle,
To breathe the fragrance of her vine and rose,
   And smoke her friendly pipe awhile.

Thence he, inspired with forecast, looked around,
   Like spies in the old Promised Land,
To search the lay of the surrounding ground,
   For milk and honey made to hand.

From Bowling Green to distant Bowerie ;
   From East to West ; from shore to shore ;
With steady tread and peerless heart did he
   The rivers, lands, and woods explore ;

Then to Gowanus crossed the placid bay,
   And all that land of fat he saw ;
And after that, on a propitious day,
   Searched out the far Communipaw :

With all so fair he knew not which to choose;
   Like bachelor mid troops of girls,
Who toss him to and fro, with many a bruise,
   From witching smiles and crumpled curls.

VII.

VOYAGE UP THE HUDSON BY SLOOP.

WHILE in this maelstrom came to his relief
   The bold and venturous *Pioneer*, —
A Knickerbocker sloop, of sloops the chief,
   In hardihood and speed and cheer.

Her old Dutch flag was flying flauntingly
   High on her thick-set, well-braced mast;
And through the streets Van Horn, of Tappan
      Zee,
   Her doughty captain, blew his blast.

He blew his blast, and cried, that " In a week,
   Or so, — within two weeks at most, —
If tide and wind proved fair, his sloop would seek
   Once more the famous Tappan coast."

Rip saw his chance, and seized it like a man ;
   By tide of fortune borne was he,
In his affairs, to lucky thought and plan,
   And settlement on Tappan Zee.

At her good hour, withouten much delay,
   Her water-cask was filled and stored ;
And all her passengers, who day by day,
   Had strolled about, now came on board.

And then the captain blew his parting blast,
   And called all hands on deck, to hoist
The sails.   Sad, parting farewells came at last,
   Through choking sobs, and eyelids moist.

Up went the sails, and out the *Pioneer*,
   By hauling, till she reached the tide ;
While Dant Van Horn stood by the helm to steer,
   With helmsman's conscious power and pride.

Captain and helmsman till the sails were filled,
   And she was fairly in the stream,
And all the landsmen's shoutings had been stilled,
   Like plaudits in a passing dream.

Then gave he, with becoming dignity,
   The helm to Hank, his trusty mate,
And like a watchful guardian of the sea,
   He paced the deck, to ward off fate.

The sloop sprung forward like an eager horse,
   When racing for a golden cup,
His body stretching forward on the course,
   His nose straight out, and tail high up ;

And well did she obey her master's will ;
    Much better than the plaguy crew ;
But in those days winds changed, as winds do still,
    And tides also, as tides now do.

'T was hence the wind chopped suddenly around,
    And hence the tide began to change ;
And hence the *Pioneer* was soon aground,
    Just opposite Weehawken range.

Meanwhile the waves went rippling by her side,
    So, that in sooth, it did appear
She still was sailing, spite of wind and tide ;
    Which kept all hands in heart and cheer.

Van Horn bragged much what speed his sloop
    could make ;
    And Rip, to see her cut and scud,
Next morn, went up on deck to watch her wake ;
    And found her sticking in the mud !

And there was yet Manhatta on the right ;
    And fair Weehawken in the west ;
And *Pioneer's* old berth still plump in sight,
    And all the world in peaceful rest.

Rip passed below and told the captain all ;
    The captain lit his pipe, and said,

With knowing wink at such a trifle small,
  The sloop last night had been to bed!

" You know," said he, " we all sometimes do that,
  And therefore cannot blame the sloop ;
Besides she 's fond of old Hoboken Flat,
  And goes there like a hen to coop.

" For that 's her native place ; there in the wood
  Her keel, and knees, and timbers grew ;
And there her bowsprit, boom, and mast once
    · stood ;
  As she well knows, and always knew.

" So with a homesick feeling, I suppose,
  Or instinct, something of that sort,
Straight for Hoboken Flat she always goes ;
  Because it is her native port.

" But wait," said he, " till she gets under way ;
  When I have waked the lazy crew ;
And we have all had breakfast, and you 'll say
  That all I 've said about her 's true.

" The fastest nag, you know, will sometimes balk,
  When driven by his native place ;
But when the tide is up you 'll see her walk,
  Like horse that chafes to run a race."

The crew at length aroused, and breakfast o'er,
　The captain blew a fearful blast,
That waked the echoes of Weehawken shore ;
　And Hank began to scratch the mast ;

And all the crew to whistle for the wind,
　By captain's orders ; and the tide
Began to flow, to suit the captain's mind ;
　Which likewise rose, with swelling pride.

Then marched all hands, by quick, well-ordered
　　tread,
　From side to side, with lusty cheer,
To rock, and rouse, and wake from cozy bed
　The drowsy, homesick *Pioneer.*

At length the waking sloop began to float ;
　And man at masthead cried, " She creeps ! "
Then stout Van Horn threw off his outer coat,
　And blew a blast to man the sweeps.

By these impelled she left her sluggish bed,
　With many a homesick sigh and groan ;
And then Van Horn began to cast the lead,
　And blast with most sonorous tone.

At first the *Pioneer* seemed bent to prove
　She *always* was a balky horse,

For she began to back, and downward move,
    Instead of forward on her course.

But by the dints of sweeps and captain's will,
    The shrew was partly tamed, and then
Yielded once more to wind and tide, and skill,
    And was quite amiable again.

She left Weehawken with its tempting glades,
    And plunging forward, on her way,
Made old Bull's Ferry, and the Palisades,
    Before sundown that breezy day.

That night she slept beneath the starry dome,
    And dreamed she stole the ebbing tide,
As she had ofttimes done, to float back home,
    And sleep at sweet Weehawken's side.

Next morn again the captain blew his blast;
    Next morn again the sturdy crew '
Whistled for wind; and Hank scraped at the
        mast;
    Till the old sloop flapped her wings and flew.

Soon Spuyten Duyvil river hove in sight;
    Then Yonkers, famous for good cheer,
Where Dant Van Horn had spent a pleasant night
    On every voyage for many a year.

That port they made, and then dropped anchor
    there,
  That all who chose might go ashore,
To breathe once more the land's refreshing air,
  And eat a landsman's meal once more.

While thus engaged the sun had sank to rest ;
  And stout Van Horn, the captain, said,
All things considered he would think it best
  To try once more a landsman's bed.

Meanwhile the yonkers from that region round,
  Who gave the town its jolly name,
Came roistering in for that they heard the sound
  Of Van Horn's blast, and knew the same.

They came to hold the ancient wrestling bout ;
  Though some, sarcastic, feigned to think
This was but cover to a wassail rout
  That gathered there to fight and drink.

Next morn the night had gone with half the crew !
  A captain 's nothing without men ;
Therefore the stout Van Horn had nought to do
  But wait till they came back again.

The second day they came, all bruised and sore,
  For they had all been somewhat thrown ;

And staggered much, as sailors do on shore ;
   And glad they were to leave that town.

From this great wrestling match the *Pioneer*,
   With streamer flying far behind,
Was wafted off, with many a yonker's cheer,
   Which aided much the prosperous wind.

For Dobbs, his ferry, pointing straight her
     nose,
   She swallowed quick the waves between ;
On which Hook Mountain gloriously arose ;
   And then the Tappan Zee was seen !

On its fair bosom hung a dreamy haze,
   Like Brussels lace on maiden's breast ;
That tended to excite the eager gaze,
   But left to fancy all the rest.

And every now and then weird Tarrytown
   Appeared, then vanished out of sight ;
Like white ghost hopping up and down ;
   Then fading into air, or light.

Young Nyack, seated on her western slope,
   Looked clean, as Holland daughters should,
And like a maiden waiting to elope
   Kept watch upon the passing flood.

These through the mist did seem but fairy guilds;
    While giant hills stood all around,
On granite ramparts, strong as Nature builds,
    To guard and ward the enchanted ground.

The tired sloop that knew these places all,
    Was filled anon with roistering mirth,
As when a horse, in sight of well-filled stall,
    Neighs, eager for his cozy berth.

The porpoises jumped round the *Pioneer*,
    Like dogs that hail their master home;
And from the farm-yard, shrill old chanticleer
    Crowed out his joy to see her come.

And soon came, gathering down upon the beach,
    Men, women, little girls and boys,
To welcome her approach within the reach
    Of their vociferated joys.

'T was then the captain brought his trumpet forth,
    With blasts that drove the mists away,
On trembling echoes, to the breezy North,
    And waked with smiles the dozing day.

Then ordered he the look-out to mast-head,
    To watch if white-caps should appear;
And Hank stood at the bows to cast the lead;
    And captain at the helm to steer.

The yawl-boat then was manned, and with a rope
　And well-pulled oars, made fast the shore ;
And ere the sun had left the grassy slope
　The good sloop's voyage was safely o'er.

That night Van Horn, upon the tavern stoop
　Rehearsed her trip, till he had shown,
To all his drowsy listeners, that the sloop
　Had *made the quickest passage known.*

VIII.

TAPPAN.

THE WAYSIDE INN.

Thus far friend Rip hath prosperous been,
　In perils by the flood ;
We only hope that on the land
　His luck may be as good.

And sure it is he did appear
　In goodly company ;
For all did love the *Pioneer*
　Who dwelt on Tappan Zee.

And he could speak Low Dutch, of course,
　Fresh from its fountain-head ;

And seemed to be a bachelor,
   Some day might wish to wed.

Nor Friendship was in those young days
   Much chary of her charms,
But threw about the stranger's neck
   Her hospitable arms.

And more than all they needed then,
   For growing State begun,
To help the population, men ;
   And our good Rip was one.

Therefore was he most welcome there,
   In ancient, brave Tappan ;
And found the latch-strings all outside,
   Because he was a man.

But Rip Van Dam, the captain bold,
   On board the *Rollicker*,
Had told him of his Tappan niece,
   And he must look for her.

Her husband kept the Wayside Inn,
   Beside the Sparkle Creek,
A homelike place, and there would Rip
   A home and lodging seek.

Her husband's name was Hans Van Horn, —
    Twin-brother born was he
Of Dant Van Horn, with whom good Rip
    Had sailed to Tappan Zee.

A mighty drinker, Hans Van Horn,
    Who kept the Wayside Inn,
And far and near was famous for
    His flips and Holland gin.

And all the country, far and near,
    For frolic and for dance,
Would gather, of a winter's night,
    In tavern kept by Hans.

And lively were the feet that pressed
    That Wayside Inn of old,
Where all the news from all around
    Was daily brought and told.

But better far for Hans Van Horn
    Had he not kept the Inn ;
And for his wife and our friend Rip
    It had far better been.

ENSCONCED and snugly housed, now Rip began
To find himself a most important man ;

Neighbors and friends he found, on every side,
Where he had thought to see a desert wide.
They came to question, and to give advice,
As neighbors always must, with judgment nice,
And offer land for sale, at any price.
No Yankee profits here, they bought it low,
And, honor bright, they meant to sell it so ;
And so they did : I wish their children did
Just long enough for me to make a bid ;
I 'd have a farm, as Rip soon found he had ;
And farms, where land is good, are not so bad.

    Rip made good use of his, as time will show ;
For time it took to fit it for the plough ;
With axe and team, with strength of arm and toil,
To clear the trees off, and to grub the soil ;
With stake and rail to quickly snake it round,
Ere first he cast the seed into the ground,
Hoping to build a fence some day to last,
When his first hurry should be overpast.
Here too the neighbors showed their kindly hearts
By coming with their stone-boats, teams, and carts,
To help the toiling Rip, and cheer him on, —
A good Dutch custom not entirely gone.
Thus scarce three months had passed ere Rip was
        cheered
By goodly stretch of land all grubbed and cleared,
And broken up, and fenced, and ploughed, and
        sowed ;

Whereat his honest heart with pleasure glowed,
And cheerful smiles upon his well-bronzed face
Did show that Labor hath his crown of grace.

MIGHTY the farmer in the days of old,
    Who cleared the forests for a glorious State ;
And laid foundations, better far than gold,
    To make her temple strong and truly great ;
    One that the people love, and tyrants hate.

He cleft the woods, to let the sunshine in ;
    He cleft the earth, to let the gold flow out ;
And riches, science, art, have ever been
    The fair dependants on his labor stout,
    Whom spangled drones regard an awkward lout.

The founders of old Rome, twin-brothers they,
    Were suckled by an old she-wolf, or bear ;
Pizarro sucked a sow, in his young day ;
    And many others who true honors wear
    Must with their honor some dishonor share.

But crowns of evergreen be on their brow
    Who rear a nation while they till the earth !
More honored they than jewelled idler now
    And evermore ; for that their toil gives birth
    To corn, and oil, and wine, and harvest mirth.

Stop we their work and all the world grows pale : ,
The factories hush their busy noise and din,
Banks tumble down, Trade stops her bartering
sale,
The wings of Commerce droop ; and pale and thin
Gaunt Famine eats the land outside and in.

The ruler and the subject, good and bad, ,
The banker, doctor, lawyer, parson, priest,
And layman, painter, poet, sane or mad, —
All the way down from greatest to the least, —
Gnawing a bone, or stuffing at a feast !

The wise, the fool, the poor, the rich, the gay,
The low, the high, the short boys and the tall,
Profane, or pious, howsoe'er they pray,
In Church and State, the great men and the
small,
Must feed on farmers, or not feed at all.

All honor then to farmers and their wives !
Long may they live, and long may they abound ;
Prolific be their labors and their lives :
May all their crops be full, and plump, and
sound,
To keep ours full, that none be empty found.

WHO has a farm must also have a house ;
  Who keeps a bird must needs possess a cage ;
Rip's longing heart sighed for his absent spouse ;
  In all his work she did his thoughts engage,
  As guardian angel of his heritage.

On Sparkle Creek he marked his homestead site,
  And first of all set out a cherry-tree,
And named it for Katrine, and morn and night,
  Ere work began, and when from labor free,
  Knelt there and prayed for her beyond the sea.

He watched it well, and nursed it with the care
  That widowed mothers show a tender child.
It scarcely drooped but seemed his life to share ;
  And day and night Katrina's spirit mild
  Came there to cheer him in the lonely wild.

The hardy burghers, with true sympathy
  For him and his Katrine, would, by and by,
Unite to build his cabin, labor free ;
  But first would finish, with the favoring sky,
  A Holy House to Him who rules on high.

That sacred work was long ago begun,
  With cheerful heart and with a ready will ;
And free-will offerings came from every one ;
  But scant their means and rude their rustic skill,
  Which left their pious toil unfinished still.

But destined soon by that industrious race,
    Complete and dedicate with prayer, to stand,
A sign devout of the supernal grace,
    Which led them through the sea by His right
        hand,
    And gave them to possess this goodly land.

Meanwhile they worshiped in the solemn grove,
    With old Dutch psalms that made the welkin
        ring,
And prayers as grateful to the Eternal Love
    As well-set phrase and song which art can bring,
    In frescoed church, to please the Almighty
        King.

The temple where they worshiped was His own;
    Not made with hands. Nor skill of man could
        raise
An edifice so worthy of His Throne
    As that where they did meet, on Sabbath days,
    To read the Word, and render prayer and praise.

The leafy roof, the mossy seat, the vine
    That hung, with clustering grapes, from oak-
        trees high,
In rich festoons, like drapery divine;
    The slanting sunlight from the open sky, —
    A symbol of the great, All-seeing Eye;

The tapering pine-tree's coned and lofty spire;
  The solemn stillness of the wilderness;
The songs of birds that mingled with the choir;
  The flowing brook, like Kedron, formed to bless
  The thirsty pilgrim, fainting with distress;

The time; the place; the quiet all around;
  The still small voice within that called them
     there;
And His great Presence, made it holy ground;
  While zephyrs poised, like angels, in the air,
  Waiting to waft to heaven their praise and
     prayer.

Such worship, in those young and earnest days,
  On holy time, in such a temple grand,
By pious men, of pure and simple ways,
  As were our fathers from the fatherland,
  Brought blessings down from Heaven's unstinted
    hand.

For " Heaven will help the men who help them-
    selves,"
  And *He will honor them who honor Him.*
Good luck comes not from stars, nor fairy elves;
  Nor can blind Fortune, with her eye-balls dim,
  Fill up our cup of pleasure to the brim.

Their cup was full, for they were well content;
  Their wants were few, and these were well sup-
      plied.
As time flew by they earned more than they
      spent;
  And with enough, and stores laid up beside,
  These simple-minded men were satisfied.

Places, and times, and tastes, have changed since
      then;
  And men have changed, and set their standard
      higher,
So that none has enough while other men
  Have more; and love of gold and pride conspire
  To burn men up with their consuming fire.

In those good times a son of Santa Claus
  Successful deemed himself, and well to do,
If he the owner of a homestead was,
  With heart and hands to work a lifetime
      through;
  Content with many acres, or a few.

His wholesome toil brought pleasant sleep at night;
  His pleasant sleep prepared him for the day;
The seasons brought him ever new delight,
  From year to year, until he passed away,
  With all his work well done, as good men may.

But now successful man means millionaire ;
   And millionaire means all a man can get,
In any way he can, by foul or fair,
   No matter how it cause his soul to fret,
   Or make his creditors and conscience sweat.

Successful man drinks all the wine he will ;
   Successful man eats more than he can bear ;
Lives in a larger house than he can fill ;
   And buys more clothes than he knows how to
      wear ;
   And swelleth much at his great bill of fare.

Successful man must bear his bags of gold,
   Through life, well-balanced on his aching head ;
Whereby he groweth bald, and gray, and old ;
   And when he dies his loving heirs, 'tis said,
   Do more rejoice than mourn that he is dead.

Successful man must leave a golden son,
   With waxen wings, to fly and bear his name,
And spend the fortune which his father won,
   Till waxen wings are melted in the flame ;
   Then sink forgotten in oblivious shame.

Is it not well to look, with longing eyes,
   On manners of the old and rugged days ?
And well their honored men once more to prize,

And seek their simple paths and pleasant ways
Where rustic virtue made their name a praise.

The fortunes which they left their growing heirs
  Were stalwart limbs, with hearts to use them
    well,
Good fathers' counsels, and good mothers' prayers,
  The tongues that knew and dared the truth to
    tell,
  And manly souls where honor loved to dwell.

These were the men who served their Maker first,
  Then helped their neighbor, helped our good
    friend Rip;
Not troubled they, like Tantalus, with thirst,
  While standing up in water to the lip,
  Which when he tried to drink gave him the slip.

Nor tortured they by *Greed*, which hungers yet,
  No matter how you stuff and cram his crop;
Which asks for more the more his cravings get;
  Nor lets his toiling slaves his feeding stop
  Till, worn to death, their hands in palsy drop.

Nor doomed to dungeons cold of *selfishness*, —
  To eat and drink in darkness and alone;
Cut off from sounds of joy and of distress,
  And every living, human chord and tone
  That tells us *Man is our own flesh and bone.*

They took their pleasure in each other's joy;
   They suffered in a brother's loss, or pain;
For others' good they gladly did employ
   Their time and toil, as free as sun and rain;
   And felt enriched at lucky neighbor's gain.

So now that gay October had begun
   To weave his many-colored robe and crown,
And that the Sacred Edifice was done,
   Rip's cabin must go up in their good town,
   Was their decree most firmly written down.

And far and wide they published the decree,
   Which far and wide no man would disobey;
So fixed the mandate, though all men were free,
   Not one in all the land would stay away,
   With willing mind, on the appointed day.

IX.

THE FROLIC.

To hew and cut the logs, and help to raise
   And build the cabin, all the neighbors came.
A Frolic this, in Knickerbocker phrase,
   A Bee, with those of Yankee blood and fame;
For work was pleasure in those early days,

As pleasure work in ours, by change of name;
So much for us the greater sin and shame.

They came from every quarter, old and young,
The stout athletic man, and robust boy;
With keen-edged axe in hand, and sharpened
tongue;
As thick as heroes at the siege of Troy,
Though not as tall. But better heroes they;—
They came to make; those others to destroy:
They came for peace; but those for bloody fray:
They came to build; those others to pull down:
Which makes material difference to a town.

From dozy Tarrytown, and Dobbs his ferry,
And Sleepy Hollow, o'er the Hudson wide,
Came many a burgher, with his Buck and Berry;
With shoulders broad, with strong and sinewy
stride,
And mirthful songs, which made the echoes merry
Leap from their caves to dance upon the tide,
And old Hook Mountain shake his shaggy side.

Scarce had the stars forsook the waning night
Ere they were up and wending on their way,
For that their toil began with early light,
And ended with the ending of the day;
Nor did neglect the morning's sacred rite,

In busy haste to reach the Frolic gay ;
Nor though they laughed did they forget to pray.

Old Tappan Zee did glory in these men,
And held her mirrors up to see their faces,
While they crossed o'er her bosom ; so that when
They somewhat looked for storms they saw no
traces
Of angry mood, though every now and then,
Their timid breakfasts changed their natural
places
For watery depths, 'mong fish of various races.

At length, by nautic skill, they reached the land,
On neighborly errand eager and intent ;
And hastening on to lend a helping hand
They waked the woods with jolly merriment ; —
A hearty and as happy rustic band
As could be gathered on a continent ; —
Old men and yonkers on the Frolic bent.

First came the Vans, the foremost men in name,
And numerous, broad, and sometimes trusty
men ;
Van Wart, in after years well known to fame ;
Van Benschoten ; Van Tassels of the glen ;
Van Hoevenburgh ; Van Schaick ; Van Bergen
(Ben) ;

The twin Van Horns, — Dant, famous for his wind,
And Hans the mighty drinker of those days ;
And following these, came, dancing, close behind,
Van Topps, whom children loved to praise ; —
Author was he of happiness to boys,
And skilled artificer of spinning-toys.
Then came Van Dyke, whose giant ancestry
Dragged half-drowned Holland, drenching, from
   the sea, —
(Nor should the pygmy bearing that great name
Obscure the effulgence of its ancient fame.)
Next Rip Van Dam, surnamed the Roarer, came, —
Amphibious he, and webbed of foot and hand ;
Van Buren next, from whom sprang Martin and
Prince John, illustrious burghers of the land.
Then the Vancliefs, Vanbliefs, and sharp Van
   Zandts,
Van Houghtens, and Van Nostrands, and Van
   Gantz,
Van Giesons, and Van Nests, and old Van Hatch ;
And broods of yonkers following, to match ;
And last Van Bung, with load of needful pans,
Closed up the rear of all the tribe of Vans.
Then came far-sighted, good Jacobus See,
Surnamed *Forecaster*, and ordained to be
The father of a numerous family.
Next him great Michael Pauw ; ancestor he
Of Huge Paws, of the fierce democracy,

And Pugilists, — (degenerate in our days);
And founder he of the illustrious town
Yclept Communipaw, in modern phrase,
But then, *Commune* of *Pauw*, of brave renown.
With him came Carl, son of the elder Carl,
And builder, in due time, of Carl his Mill;
Then Barnes the blacksmith, famous for the snarl
In which he got, at trial of his skill
At quoits, with doughty Peek, at Peek his Kiln;
Then last, from Sleepy Hollow, in the rear,
Well known for reticence and quiet cheer,
Came Knapp, inventor of the easy chair
And home-made lounges stuffed with husks of
      corn,
Hatcheled like flax, to save the cost of hair;
Renowned for these, but most of all renowned
As first male child in Sleepy Hollow born,
And lineal descendant, son, and heir
Of the Patroon of that enchanted ground, —
Van Dozen Knapp, its great discoverer.
    These joined the Nyackers, with loud hurras,
And other doughty and huge-lifting men,
Who came, with solid tramp, from hill and glen,
All armed with crowbars, chains, and iron claws;
The Mildoberghers, Rosencranz, and Frees;
The mighty Millspaughs, builders they of dams;
The Dunspaughs, — town collectors; Minnerlys, —
Great hunters they of squirrels, great on clams,

Wild-pigeons, and the run of shad ; the Keese ;
The Hammonds, famous for the cure of hams ;
The Boise, Duboise, the De Bevoise, and Claus ;
The Hasbroucks, Snedekers, and Monelaus.
    Such were the mighty men who came to build
And lay foundation for Van Bigham's house,
With generous heart and lofty purpose filled,
To bring from Faderland his absent spouse.
    O happy Nation ! happy family !
And every tribe and clan below the skies !
And almost every one, on land, or sea,
That has a head proportioned to his size !
That will and purpose, plan and policy,
May keep the hands and feet from anarchy.
    The folks of Tappan Zee in this were wise.
From all their weightiest men they picked out two
Who were preëminent in weight and size,
Either of whom for Head would surely do ; —
The one from Nyack, one from Tarrytown,
'Twixt whom to choose their Ruler, Head, and
      Guide,
For all that busy day till sun went down ;
Then to the steel-yard balance hung them each ;
And weighed them fairly ; standing all aside,
Lest some designing hand might overreach,
And turn the scales in favor of his choice ;
And he who weighed the most received their
      voice

And vote, unanimous, with loud acclaim ;
Shouting and yelling forth their leader's name.
    The conquered candidate was Rick Dubois ;
The conqueror, Diedrich Scraalenburgh, the scribe ;
Who weighed the most, ten pounds avoirdupois,
So he was chosen Ruler of the tribe.
    Undue proportion was his only fault ;
He was most perfect in his appetite,
But showed the bulging pressure of much malt ;
Was willing every dog should have his bite,
And every tired man from work should halt :
He always knew that he was always right :
Born to command, he loved preëminence ;
And had he not grown broader than his length,
And waddled in his walk ; and had his sense
Kept equal pace with his great size and strength,
And had his stomach not outgrown his head,
In disproportion vast and cumbersome, —
Their chosen chief, as they most truly said,
So great his will, might easily have clomb
To any height ambition bade him come !
But circumstances, owing to his size,
And love of malt, had ordered otherwise.
    The Great Elect stood forth, with modest pride,
And took the helm of power, intent to guide
All other wills, as Frolic laws provide ; —
That no two forces pull in opposite ways,
The log with ox-team hitched at either end ;

And none stand idle, with a puzzled gaze,
Not knowing where a helping hand to lend.
    He mounting on a cart-tail for a throne,
With ox-goad for a sceptre, gave commands, —
The chosen Head with doughty tongue and tone,
To ready feet and willing, toiling hands ;
And set the times when they should take a drink,
And smoke their pipes, and breathe the teams
      awhile.
As with the body 't is the head must think
For all the lower parts ; in some such style
The common people needs must have a Head,
To do their thinking, work their wisdom out,
Or show a due authority instead ; —
With chosen policy for learned and lout ; —
That hands and feet may know what they're about.
    These all obeyed, and did their several work :
No sluggards there ; but hearty and alive :
None wished to spare himself, nor tried to shirk ;
Nor was a drone in all that busy hive
Of men, whose rule was, They *who work shall*
      thrive.
    The ready trees scarce waited for the axe
Ere, falling quick, they came, well-trimmed and
      straight,
To test the strength of sturdy Dutchmen's backs.
(Log-rolling is an easier craft of late,
And source of honor, both in Church and State.)

Down from the craggy woods with easy grade,
The logs are snagged ; and all the yielding soil
Is marked by ridges which their courses made,
Like honest wrinkles on the face of toil :
And soon all notched, in row on row, are laid
At the selected site, by Sparkle Brook.
    The cellar, opened by the delving spade,
Receives its rough stone walls, with cheery look ;
While far and near the peaceful vale rebounds
With Labor's quick, reverberating sounds ;
And all the air of bright October seems
Alive with voices, speaking to their teams.
The scolding squirrels stop chattering in the tree,
And look to learn what all the noise can be ;
And then berate the workmen saucily !
The watching quails, perplexed by strange new
        fates,
Whistle their signal-notes, to warn their mates ;
And in reply the signs each imitates.
The crows are cawing at camp-meeting rates,
Foretelling new corn-fields, with wealth of food,
And much rejoice, as prophets of the wood
And hungry, happy, black-coat preachers should
Who wear such sable garbs, at coming good.
    Thus for a season all passed peacefully ;
As busy hive, directed by queen-bee,
Or noisy brooklet, running to the sea ;
For work and mirth embracing, tripped along,
As instruments keep time with vocal song.

Then suddenly a little breeze arose,
Like murmurings of the brewing of a storm ;
And soon the cloud assumed a giant form.
Like great from small, it grew from Diedrich's
    nose ;
This lacked the natural bridge, whose arch-like
    swells
Kind Nature makes to hold one's spectacles ;
Hence Diedrich's often gave his nose the slip,
Nor rested till they reached its fiery tip :
And so it came to pass, while in this plight,
He saw things in a double sort of light : —
The logs which first seemed large anon looked
    small,
And here and there were some not seen at all.
Thereby some strange mistakes had just occurred,
Which some one hinted with a timid word ;
And this changed Diedrich's smile into a frown ;
And this built Rip's log-cabin *upside down !*
Bad sign, said they, who gabbled of such signs, —
Van Giesons chief of these, and Landerines.
" Do as I say ! " the doughty Leader said,
" Let not the Hands rebel against the Head ! "
Then broad foundation-logs were topmost laid ;
And those that should be topmost underneath.
Great Diedrich's wrath, like broadsword from its
    sheath,
Leaped from his choleric stomach, sharp and quick.
They saw it coming, heard its fearful click,

As from its depths it sprang ; nor waited they
To feel its edge, but hastened to obey.
    But still his wrath poured forth ; an oath it bore
Which turned the cabin round, back side before,
And brought the gable-end close to the road !
And still he raged.   Shaking his huge ox-goad
He thus addressed the awe-struck Frolickers : —
" Who is it dares to contravene my word ?
My will ? my Policy ? you stubborn curs !
Can I not see ?   Do I not bear the sword ?
Are eyes for nothing ?   These nigh logs, I know,
Are much the larger.   Do I not know logs ?
Have I not rolled and rolled them, many a day ?
How dare you then affirm it is not so ?
Can I not tell young sucking-pigs from hogs ?
The big from little ?   Go to work ! I say :
Don't contradict, but listen and obey !
What is the Head for but to have his way ?
I 'll put it to the people ! — they agree
That I shall carry out my Policy.
I 'm here to rule ; and boys ! for mercy sakes,
Don't rile me with your blundering mistakes ! "
'T was vain to hint about his failing eyes,
And slippery spectacles, — that just before
He 'd ordered these same logs contrariwise ;
That he was one, and they at least three-score ;
And sixty pair of eyes were better than
The single pair of any living man :

A live volcano was his burning wrath,
Which only poured forth fiery words the more,
The more they tried to turn or dam its path.
When cool, their blunders filled him with surprise ;
His eyes were worth a thousand other eyes !
With such a pair of specs to help his sight!
And what he knew he knew, — knew he was right ;
He hated stubbornness, that dreadful evil,
As much as common men could hate the devil.

'T was thus by Diedrich's wrathful will and frown
That Rip Van Bigham's house was upside down.
And thus by that huge, mighty oath he swore
Rip's house was turned about, hindside before ;
And by the shaking of his great ox-goad
The gable-end stood plump against the road.
Thus oft doth right succumb to mighty wrong,
Through lack of power to help itself along.

The gable-end so tickled all the vrouws
It soon became the rage for every house ;
And Fashion spread her mandates far and wide,
Till gable-ends were signs of taste and pride,
Down Hudson's glorious river, side by side,
As far as Gotham and Communipaw ;
And up the river far as good Dutch law
And good Dutch sloops with safety could ascend,
The rage prevailed for Diedrich's gable-end, —
A fashion born of freak, and not intent,
Like great discoveries made by accident.

And Fashion makes amends for many sins,
And in the end both wise and foolish wins.
  But nothing good has ever yet been known
From Rip's log-cabin being upside down ;
And Diedrich's nose has much to answer for,
As cause, though small, of mighty ills it bore.
Bad sign, to start with, when a house is made
Without foundation well and wisely laid.
Its upper works are weak and ill-secure,
And all between is neither safe nor sure,
But topsy-turvy, with confusion wed,   •
The house seems always standing on its head.
  Alas ! the signs proved true ; they came to pass.
Alas, for Rip ! for human hopes, alas !
In those old times when witches rode the air,
And ghosts came out to walk the earth at night,
When nightmare-tramps were neither few nor
        fair ;
When death-ticks, and the fearful second-sight,
And goblin freaks were common everywhere ;
They more prevailed in country than in town,
But most of all in houses upside down.
  So in our times, and in a similar way,
When devils are allowed a holiday,
And evil spirits, long in limbo pent,
Come back to earth, " to see the elephant,"
They all with one consent, for quarters, seek
The crazy house whose corner-stone is weak,

Or whose foundations are mere cobble-stones.
At these they knock their skeleton knuckle-bones;
In them they hold their weird and revel-rout;
Their tables turn, — turn Hades inside out;
Tell them the secrets of the burning marl,
To put the peaceful family in a snarl;
And let them see, by special friendly boon,
What most men fear they 'll see and know too
    soon.
  And fierce chained angels, let out on paroles
Of honor, from their prison-pens in hell,
For respite from the work of torturing souls,
And few days' sport with mortals, love to dwell
In homes like these until their time is up; —
Eat at their tables, drink the self-same cup;
Sleep in their garrets, cellars, empty rooms;
And telegraph, by knocks, men's hidden dooms;
Tell lies and grin like imps through these kind
    friends
As medium; till the farce, or worse thing ends;
Then back again to Hades, there to burn,
And wait a visit from their friends in turn.

  But why anticipate the troublous day,
In the dim distance, still so far away?
Why in the sunshine dread the future storm
Which robes in light its dark and misty form?

Rip's house went up, and that was something
    gained ;
Though somewhat awkward-built and rudely paned ;
And all that day the bright October sun
Smiled on the work kind hearts and hands had
    done ;
Nor sank to rest until he saw the roof
Completely on, and almost water-proof ;
And a huge chimney standing out to guard,
As faithful sentinel, the house and yard ; —
This done he slept, first putting out his light,
And snored on golden pillows all the night.
Then had the Dutchmen done a good day's toil,
And they too rested ; cleansing first the soil
From honest hands as Nature ever made,
To rear a house, or hold a plough or spade.

    Good Rip was thanking them, in simple speech,
But more by looks than what his tongue could say ;
For all his words seemed loitering by the way, —
As if their journey's end they 'd never reach, —
When shrill the conch-horn sounded forth the
    feast, —
The Frolic-feast, succeeding Frolic-work.

    The noontide meal that day, for man and beast,
Was stout but short ; the evening's none will shirk ;
Each feels the place where appetite doth lurk.
October hung out all his evening stars ;

The Dutchmen hung out pine-knots, here and there,
Along the boards that stretched o'er crotch and
      bars,
The smoking wealth of that great meal to bear,
For hungry host, in brisk and bracing air.
The juicy viands gave a savory smell,
Uprising through cross-bars of puffy dough ;
The art of meat-pies good Dutch vrouws knew well:
It was a marvel how they browned them so !
And there they stood, all piping row on row.
No wonder that few words, beside the grace,
Were spoken for a season, by the men ;
For insubstantial things must need give place
To substance ; and what use of language when
Actions speak louder far, as theirs did then ?
The men who work not neither shall they eat ;
But men who work shall earn and eat the best,
And sleep of working men is sound and sweet.
And they of all men are most truly blest,
And readiest they of all to go to rest.

    Happy the man who has good work to do,
And does it all as well as he knows how !
True to his Master, to his conscience true,
He at the last, with sun-set on his brow,
Can say, *My work is done, I'll rest me now.*

    Then shall he sleep, and sweet shall be his rest ;
As when in glory sinks the setting sun
Down on the golden pillows of the west,

For he shall reap the fruits his toil has won,
And hear the Master say to him, " Well done ! "

    At length their tongues were freed, and floating
        round
From joke to joke, from story to a song,
On this great quest they ran themselves aground.
" How can a farmer help himself along ? "
" What duty stands the foremost on a farm, —
The chief to be observed, on wisest plan,
Thereby to guard himself from loss and harm,
Thereby to come out a successful man ? "

VAN TASSEL said, The first great thing
Of which a man should think or sing,
That he may wealth and fortune bring,
        Is cattle.
The one thing needful on a farm
Is this, — to keep well housed and warm,
Well-fed, and sheltered from the storm,
        The cattle.
One thought to keep the fences up,
Another to avoid the cup,
And rise at daylight with the lark,
And keep things snug, and toe the mark,
        Was half the battle.

Van Buren said that change of seed,
And frequent hoeing was the need.
Fat Pruyn affirmed, to feed the land,
Like cattle, with a liberal hand,
And keep it fat, was just the thing
To make a farmer's purse to ring;
For farms, like cows, the more you feed,
The more they 'll give you, deed for deed.

———

At length spake Rip, the honored host: —
  " All you have said is wise ;
But what I think is needed most
  Came not in your replies.

" For what are lands and cattle worth,
  Or house and gardens fair,
If she we love the most on earth
  Be absent from us there ?

" The fairest lands are desolate,
  The house an empty house,
And drear and lone the best estate,
  Without a loving spouse.

" What was the earth till came the sun
  The darkness to relieve ?

And what, when Paradise was done,
    Was Eden without Eve ?

" Therefore, I think the first great care
    Of every farmer's life,
At home, abroad, and everywhere,
    Should be to please his wife."

This brought a song from old Van Benschoten ;
    Though strong his limbs his voice was rather
        frail ;
And if we believe his son, the younger Ben,
    " It quivered like a sliver on a rail. "

OUR WIVES.

LET others sing of girls they love,
    Or praise their lands and houses ;
Our song shall be of riper fruit,
    And richer gold, — our spouses !

For what were girls, or boys, or both,
    And what were lands and houses ;
And what were gold, or life itself,
    Without our buxom spouses !

We loved them well when they were young,
    The thought our fancy rouses ;

But though as sweethearts much we loved,
   We love them most as spouses !

What would our homes be did not they
   Clean up, and mend our trousers ;
And soon the world would empty be
   If 't were not for the spouses !

THE GIRLS.

Young Rick Van Nest thought otherwise ;
   But blushed when asked to sing ;
He thought the girls had brighter eyes,
   And brighter every thing.

" From whence," said he, " do spouses come,
   To cheer your old men's lives,
If not from girls, who leave their home
   To be the young men's wives ?

" From whence the good, ripe fruits, that bring
   The joy of winter hours,
But from the spring-time blossoming,
   And early summer flowers ?

" As sure as swelling rivers flow
   From little brooks and waters,
So sure the best of good vrouws grow
   From best of little daughters ! "

Then called they for Brommy, the sunny
    Brom Lippencott, easy and free,
To tell them a story funny,
    Or to sing for them merrily.

He'd come from old Spuyten Duyvil,
    To marry on Tappan Zee,
And laughed in the face of his rival,
    Had Brom Lippencott, said he.

Therefore, he would sing them a sober,
    Gay song, if such there could be ;
And the song should be of October,
    For reasons they shortly should see.

For the month that makes the world mellow
    And pockets the golden corn,
Was to marry the happiest fellow
    To the prettiest girl ever born.

Then Lippencott sang of October,
    In a full, manly voice sang he ;
And the voices of evening sober
    Chimed in with a merry glee :

OCTOBER.

LIKE Joseph, son of Jacob old,
    All gayly clothed, though sober,

And by his elder brethren sold,
    Is glorious, gay October !

He garners grain for time of need,
    And bids all men remember
In plenteous months to take good heed
    For barren, scarce December.

Clad like a king in regal state,
    According to the story,
Next to the King good Joseph sate,
    And next to him in glory.

But first of months, of all the year,
    Though subject and right loyal,
October wears a kingly gear,
    And crown of glory royal.

The Summer leaves her sweetest charm
    For the face of bright October ;
And so his smiles are always warm,
    Although his brow is sober.

And then to heal the Summer ills,
    Jack Frost comes with his vetoes
Against the vile obnoxious bills
    Of vermin and mosquitoes.

6

By day the quails, for our delight,
　　Are whistling in the stubble;
And katydids sing half the night,
　　To drive away our trouble.

We throw our clubs up in the trees,
　　And down the chestnuts rattle!
And faster fall, and better please,
　　Than bullets in a battle.

The 'prentice boy, with master's gun,
　　Goes forth for a day's adventure;
And if he gets no other fun,
　　Gets a day from his indenture.

The squirrel leaps from tree to tree,
　　As if his wits had quit him;
Then pops his tail up just to see
　　If 'prentice boy can hit him.

The days are warm, the nights are cool,
　　Just fit to make us rollic,
And dance at work, at play, or school,
　　Or at Van Bigham's frolic.

There's not a lady in the land,
　　However wealth caress her,

With silks and satins at command,
 And waiting-maids to dress her, —

Try as she may, and do her best,
 Use what she will to robe her,
With jewels and gold from East and West,
 Can dress like gay October,

If he appears from boots to crown,
 As we have ever found him,
In purple, crimson, yellow, and brown,
 His robes of glory round him;

Or if all lands of earth we try,
 And islands of the ocean ;
Or if from world to world we fly,
 With wings for locomotion, —

We could not find beneath the sky,
 On our revolving globe, or
On globes of light, in realms on high,
 A month like our October !

HOME AND TO BED.

The old Dutch beds in our forefather's times,
Like some at the times I am writing,

With pillows of down, and snowy white sheets,
   And so forth, were very inviting.

Their home-woven counterpanes, quilts of patch-
      work,
   And feather-beds piled like a mountain,
With every thing clean as a fresh-opened rose,
   Of sleep and good dreams were the fountain.

And a good day's hard work, as their work had
      been,
   And a hearty, good supper thereafter,
Topped off with a joke and a song, and all that
   To help their digestions with laughter,

Prepared the good fellows, though fast-grappled
      friends,
   For the shaking of hands and the parting,
While Berrys and Bucks were as willing as they
   For the cracking of whips and the starting.

Good-by! They are gone, and will soon be at
      home,
   With their good vrouws, the Marthas and Marys;
And Rip's log cabin looks lonesome enough,
   In the woods, with the sylvan fairies.

X.

THE EMPTY HOUSE.

TIME, with his great revolving wheel,
　　Turned Autumn off, brought Winter round;
And Winter placed his icy heel,
　　With clanging tramp, upon the ground.

He smote the earth with angry hand;
　　Earth moaned away its dying breath;
A shroud fell from the unknown land,
　　And covered its cold form of death.

The village inn gave noisy mirth;
　　But Rip sat brooding in his gloom,
And skies, that mourned the buried earth,
　　Cast shadows in his silent room.

The storm-winged months passed slowly now;
　　And lagging, seemed so many years;
While clouds hung heavy, on his brow,
　　With strange presentiments of fears.

Three months ago his house was done,
　　And he had written to Katrine;
Ere yet the clouds obscured the sun,
　　Or earth's white winding-sheet was seen.

No dolorous thought escaped him then,
    But words that hope and love impart,
Flowed cheerily from his gentle pen
    To call his loved one to his heart.

RIP'S LETTER.

DEAR WIFE: I take my pen in hand,
    Once more, to write that " all is well."
I want to see you, dear Katrine,
    Far more than I have words to tell.

Our house is ready, — built of logs
    Rough-hewn, — not large, nor very small;
But airy, strong, and snug, and warm; —
    Much better than no house at all.

'T will be a *Home when you are here,*
    But not a day before you come;
No place on earth, however dear,
    Without you could appear like home.

I seem to have floated on a tide
    Of sun-lit waves, all swift and strong,
So prosperous have I been, dear Kate;
    And yet the time seems very long.

Time, since we parted, seems an age,
   And yet as fresh as yesterday ;
'T was always short when you were near,
   And always long with you away.

You 'll like this new world, dear Katrine, —
   I do believe that heaven and earth
And ocean must have done their best
   To give this glorious country birth !

And heaven and earth must have combined
   To fit the people for the land ;
I know it by my neighbors here,
   So kind are they in heart and hand.

This poor man's country, where he finds
   A rich reward for honest toil,
Can have no rival on the globe,
   With brighter skies or richer soil.

Could we have known as much before
   We parted as since then I 've seen,
The ocean would not now divide
   Our empty house and my Katrine.

But every thing is for the best ;
   And love, that taught us to endure,
Will help us hope and bear the rest ;
   For love's reward is ever sure.

I 'm lonely here without you, Kate,
　　But would be lonely anywhere ;
A crowded town were desolate
　　If you were absent from me there.

And I could love the wilderness,
　　Or live in deserts wild and rude,
If my Katrine were there to bless
　　And cheer me, in the solitude.

My thoughts oft bear me far away,
　　Till we are standing, side by 'side,
In the old church, that happy day
　　That blessed me with a blushing bride.

And while I write, my fancy brings
　　You here, as it has often brought ; —
I wish the *Rollicker* had wings,
　　To go and come as quick as thought !

But I 'll be patient yet and wait,
　　And busy work shall make time fly,
Until we meet, — till then, dear Kate,
　　I 'm yours, and yours until I die.

MUCH more he wrote which but pertains
　　To loving hearts like theirs, I ween ;
And much too sacred for the eye
　　Of any but his own Katrine.

With this he reached Manhattan Isle,
　　On board the swift sloop *Pioneer*,
And gave it to his friend, Van Dam,
　　Stout captain of the *Rollicker*.

The Captain listened to his plan,
　　While to his care committed he
The treasure of his heart, Katrine,
　　To bring her safely o'er the sea.

To which good Rip Van Dam agreed,
　　With all a sailor's generous heart, —
Saying he had a wife himself,
　　From whom 't was hard to live apart.

And he had known Katrine and Rip
　　Since they were children, long ago ;
And he would bring her safely o'er,
　　Unless the winds forgot to blow.

And you can trust the *Rollicker*,
　　For what she is your eyes have seen !
You found her safe for you, my boy !
　　You'll find her safe for your Katrine.

Rip answered, that he knew the ship,
　　And knew her doughty Captain brave ;
And for himself would never fear,
　　In such good hands, the wind or wave ;

But somehow timid felt for her, —
    He knew not why, unless that she
Had always, from her childhood, felt
    An inward horror of the sea.

" And yet I know you 'll bring her safe.
    So, Captain, take good care of her!
And He who rules the winds and waves
    Will bless the good ship *Rollicker*."

Thus spake good Rip, and away and away
Flew the ship on the wings of the wind :
Her own wings were strong and white ;
And Hope, like an angel of light,
Took the helm, in Rip's swift mind,
And guided her night and day, —
And guided her day and night, —
Till the sea, that lay between
His empty house and Katrine,
Was crossed and recrossed by the ship ;
And he pressed her to his heart,
And kissed the love from her lip
Never! no, never again to part!

Thus flew the ship in Bigham's thought,
    Swifter than words could tell,
The ship that oft the storms had fought,
    And oft had won, as well.

A better ship could not be found !
   In sooth, a ship was she,
From stem to stern all safe and sound,
   And good as ship could be.

From stem to stern, from deck to keel,
   All firmly knit and strong ;
Broad in the girth, but true as steel,
   Worthy the sailor's song !

But thought is swifter than a ship,
   However fast she be ;
And Rip's quick thought had made the trip
   Ere she had crossed the sea.

Fair was the wind, the sea was smooth,
   And calm, from shore to shore ;
Such voyage the Captain said, in sooth,
   He never made before.

But when she neared the dear home-port
   Of Amsterdam the old,
A cloud was seen, of evil sort,
   That feared the Captain bold.

It settled on good Barthold's home,
   The father of Katrine,
Foretelling evil days to come,
   By sign too often seen, —

By sign Van Dam had known, alas!
   And Rip would know too soon;
For grief would surely come to pass
   When clouds appeared at noon.

THE MESSENGERS.

THE ship was safely moored; and in due time
   Discharged her cargo; and obediently
Awaited orders to reseek the clime,
   When duty called, the other side the sea.

Meantime Van Dam had sought the fair Katrine,
   With happy word that Rip had bid him come
To fetch her to the home she ne'er had seen, —
   A humble, but, with her, a happy home.

Good news, alas! do sometimes come too late!
   Had this been told Katrine some weeks before
It might have saved her from the coming fate
   That called her to another distant shore.

The hope deferred, the longing heart, and fears
   That Rip was lost in the great storm at sea,
Were fuel for the fever which her tears
   Had never quenched when flowing copiously.

But these had dried; and then the fever raged
   With inward flame that burned her life away;

Nor skill long tried its fury had assuaged,
    While aught remained to burn, from day to
        day.

And now she lay like wreck upon the tide,
    Where counter winds and currents hold it
        fast ;
Now swayed to this, now to the other side,
    Till favoring breezes blow, or fatal blast.

Too late ! too late ! the love-born zephyrs blew
    On Barthold's house, where the dark cloud was
        seen ;
Van Dam had not yet entered ere he knew
    Its shadow rested on the fair Katrine.

The Captain found a house of mourning there ;
    Another messenger had come before,
To call her to another world more fair,
    A home more fair than Hudson's glorious
        shore,
    To which her husband called with longing heart
        and sore.

She scarcely breathed ; bright angels, o'er her
        bending,
    With fragrant wings, were there to help her fly ;
The soul, like air, grows pure by its ascending,

And hers was pure, for she was near the sky ;
And they who looked on her did think it joy to
    die.

A holy man of God, a pure and simple man,
    Knelt down and they all bowed in humble
      prayer ;
And then, in glowing words, he showed the plan
    Of grace divine, by which our Lord did bear
    The cross for all who in his cross and crown will
      share.

" Who bear the cross the crown shall also wear ; "
    And she, the sweet Katrine, had long ago
Secured of both the cross and crown her share !
    Already she had passed all sin and woe ;
    And soon her soul would shine in heaven's
      effulgent glow.

The path that ends in glory must begin
    Low down, in sweet humility of place ;
Like His, the manger who was laid within,
    Who died upon the cross for human race,
    And now in glory reigns, with majesty and
      grace.

THE PATH.

HARD by a valley,
 Shaded and deep,
Riseth a mountain,
 Rugged and steep.

Narrow a pathway,
 Dim to the eye,
Threadeth the mountain,
 Reacheth the sky.

Low in the valley
 Standeth a gate,
Fronting the pathway,
 Narrow and strait.

Few there be enter it,
 Stooping so low ;
Small is the number
 Heavenward go.

Pride passeth by it,
 Scorneth the gate, —
Finds it too narrow,
 Finds it too strait.

Selfishness, vanity,
 Babbling philosophy,
Worldly insanity,
 Swelling morality,

Sceptical Sadducee,
 Infidel hate,
Self-righteous Pharisee,
 Scoff at the gate!

Only the humble,
 Grieving for sin,
Halt by the gate-way,
 Enter within.

Angels, like sunbeams,
 Downward descending,
Smile on the pathway
 Heavenward tending.

Rugged the climbing;
 Danger each side;
But with the pilgrim
 Angels abide.

Pointing him upward,
 Showing his crown,

Strengthening, cheering,
  Helping him on.

All the path pleasant,
  Fragrant, though steep ;
All its tears dew-drops
  Sweet flowers weep.

All the sky smiling
  Storm-clouds above ;
All the air musical,
  Laden with love.

Onward and upward,
  Ever ascending,
Soon with the sky-robes
  His will be blending!

Earth far below him,
  Fading away ;
Nearer and clearer
  Shineth the day!

Earth far below him,
  Heaven in sight, —
Lo! he has vanished
  Into its light!

Thus spake the Preacher, in a gentle voice ;
　　Not for her sake who all unconscious lay,
But that the sorrowing friends might then rejoice,
　　As they beheld her on the shining way !

Then took their harps, which hope and faith had
　　　strung,
　　This gathered company of mourning friends,
And in low tones of solemn music sung
　　Of that bright world where this swift journey
　　　ends.

For when Death's wing comes down, like evening's
　　　gloom,
　　It falls not on the dying one alone !
Each feels himself borne onward to the tomb,
　　And in the dying face beholds his own.

THE HYMN.

(HEAVENWARD BOUND.)

TIME is rushing in his chariot ;
　　Rapidly his wheels go round ;
Though they cast no dust behind them,
　　Though they leave no rumbling sound ;
Silently they bear us onward ;
　　Soon our journey will be o'er ;

Soon the friends with whom we mingle
   We shall see and hear no more ;
Soon our feet shall press the meadows
   Of the vast eternal shore.

Flying months and years remind us
   Of the world we 're passing to ;
Let us leave good deeds behind us,
   In the world we 're passing through,
Which shall be the seeds of kindness,
   Watered by celestial dew ;
And shall bear good fruits for others,—
   Fruits of joy and peace and love,
Years long after we are singing
   In the immortal land above.

Men are born, and men are dying;
   Thousands come, not one can stay ;
Time is swift, his wheels are flying,
   Never ceasing, night nor day,
For the laughter, nor the crying
   Of the stricken or the gay ;
Crushing down the God-defying, —
   They who laugh at Death's delay ;
And from sorrow, sin, and sighing
   Bearing gentle souls away.

Plans and schemes of men and nations;
   Hearts and homes and homestead-tree

Granite walls and Art's creations,
  All the eye delights to see,
All the ear delights in hearing,
  Crumble, tumble, fall and fade!
Oh! we need a world more cheering,
  Free from graves and cypress shade:
Thanks to God! that world we 're nearing,
  In eternal sapphires laid.

Weeks passed.   Katrina lived, though scarce
    alive;
The blood forsook her face, and marble came
With living flesh for mastery to strive;
Her eyes were closed, her tongue spake but one
    name;
And the cold waves of death strove with life's
    feeble flame.

The day had come on which she was to sail
For the New World, beyond the swelling tide.
Alas! the ship would carry woe and wail
To Bigham's heart, in place of happy bride,
For whom he waited with such longing love and
    pride.

The ship delayed that the good Captain might
Take word decisive of Katrina's fate.
He left her dying-bed at twelve of night,

Agreeing on a signal, which should state,
At dawn, if she had passed the dark and dolorous
    gate.

The signal was a winding-sheet, waved from
The house-top, if Katrine that night should die.
Alas! he saw it waving from her home,
Whose light grew dark as light sprung up the sky,
Next morn, at early dawn. Alas, the reason why!

With this sad news, a heavy freight of grief,
The ship, with sagging sails, dropped down the
        stream;
Nor from the mournful burden felt relief
Till smiling Ocean's vast and glorious gleam
Dispelled it, as the day dispels a frightful dream.

THE BLESSED DEAD.

Mournfully, rejoicingly,
    We look upon the dead;
Glad that the happy soul has passed
    The boundaries we dread;
Sad for the house whose darkened walls
    Sigh for the spirit fled.

Mournfully, rejoicingly,
    We close the loving eyes;

Sad for the loss of their dear light
    Which made home Paradise ;
But glad that they do now behold
    Their Maker, in the skies.

Mournfully, rejoicingly,
    We see the smile, so meek,
Now fixed upon the pleasant lips,
    Alas ! that will not speak !
We weep, and yet rejoice that she
    Still smiles, though we are weak.

Mournfully, rejoicingly,
    We bear the dead away ;
Sad for the living beauty gone
    From that most wondrous clay ;
But glad to know 't will rise again,
    In Life's immortal day.

Mournfully, rejoicingly,
    Not hopelessly and vain,
We send our tears and prayers to God,
    That He will heal our pain ;
Sad that our world has lost so much,
    Glad for what Heaven doth gain.

XI.

BAD NEWS.

Bad news flies swiftly on the east wind's wings;
And while good Rip Van Bigham, faithful man,
Good husband, living only for Katrine,
Toiling for her, and forming every plan,
With eager hope already saw her near,
And every lagging day stretched to a week,
The swift-winged *Rollicker*, with tidings drear,
Brought pangs of death, to slay his loving heart.

Van Dam, the kind good Captain, came himself,
With softest words, and wise considerate art,
To break by slow degrees the dreadful blow.

A thunderbolt, from brightest noon-day sky
Fell, crashing! when the gentle sailor spake.
Poor Rip was dumb with horror.   Not a sigh
Escaped him.   Not a word he uttered then;
But dumb and breathless, like as if to die;
Till good Van Dam seized hold his death-like
        hand
And gently said, — "Rip! we must act like
        men!"
Then burst the pent-up shower; tears fell like
        rain,
And with a long, deep groan he lived again.
He lived, but all he lived for on the earth

Was gone. The life that made his life was gone.
The roots were gone that gave its blossoms birth.
He moved like an automaton, a form,
Without the vital energy of man, —
A wreck at mercy of the driving storm.
Plans, hopes, home, joy, all wrecked at once !
The pangs of parting, exile, toil, in vain ;
His long, sweet dream of life all turned to pain.
The sun went out and left him to the night;
And night was drowned in tears, and gave no
     stars.
Alike to him night's gloom or midday light ;
The earth was iron, and the heavens were brass ;
And life a worthless, useless thing below ;
And man seemed made for wretchedness and woe.
    Death cast his shadow on all living things,
And shook his skeleton fingers, night and day,
With hour-glass waiting but the hour to strike,
And all things waited merely for their doom.
How strange that men kept toiling wearily on !
That all the world was busy, mid the gloom !
Nothing to him was good on earth but sorrow ;
Nothing he hoped for half so much as death ;
For this he prayed with every evening's breath,
That he might sleep and wake not with the mor-
     row.
And when the morrow came, with morning's light,
He prayed that he might die before the night.

But that dark gate, that led to his Katrine,
Was closed against him.   And his earthly home
Was closed and dark; for she had passed away;
And hope across its threshold could not come.
A homesick exile in a weary world,
The future blank before him night and day,
In love with grief, and loving solitude,
He sought the shadows of the lonely wood,
And plunged in darkness of the wilderness.

    Nor passed into the wilderness alone;
No man can be alone; though none may see
What bright-winged guardians keep him company,
Who have the charge of mortals in distress.
The angel sought him out, and soothed him there;
Touched his cold hand with hand most heavenly
       fair;
And led him forth from darkness to the light,
And set him down beneath the cherry-tree,
Which, strange to say, drooped not with winter's
       blight.

    With zephyr whispers there recounted he,
As if from well-stored, loving memory,
Of him and his Katrine, their childhood's days;
Their school-day tasks, their merry plays,
Their early love, its tender forming leaf,
Its fragrant blossoming without a grief;
Their marriage, parting, hopes, and human fears,
And smiles and tears all ending now in tears.

Then, pointing upward through the sky between
The weeping husband and his dead Katrine,
Asked, " Would you call her, were the power
    given,
Back to this weary world from yon bright heav-
    en ? "
Good Rip was silent; but his heart said, " No ! "
E'en while his lips were silent with his woe.
Thus was the good man, in his sore distress,
By angels strengthened in the wilderness.

ANGELS.

ANGELS have passed 'twixt earth and heaven,
    Unseen by mortal eyes,
E'er since our stricken race were driven
    By sin from Paradise ;
They make no rustling of the wing,
Nor can we hear the songs they sing.

Swift as the light they come and go,
    On some mysterious plan,
Touched by the sight of human woe,
    In pitying love for man ;
We know they come, but cannot trace
Their pathway through the shining space.

Down from the heavenly hills on high
    To earth's far-distant plain,
Where prostrate millions groan and die,
    With poisoned arrows slain,
In loving haste, they fly to bring
The healing balm upon their wing.

To babes who in their cradles weep,
    They whisper, soft and low,
And soothe the little ones to sleep,
    With glory on their brow;
Then bear them gently to the skies,
To bloom like buds in Paradise.

Where tears of humble sorrow flow
    From broken hearts for sin;
Where lilies of the valley grow,
    We know their steps have been;
They come to bear the flower and gem
To deck the Saviour's diadem.

Where wounded pilgrims press the ground,
    Or faint beneath their load,
The winged Samaritans are found,
    All timely, on the road,
To bathe their wounds with oil and wine,
Brought with them from the Land divine.

And when a good man shuts his eyes,
Bidding the world farewell,
They wait to bear him to the skies,
With joy no tongue can tell ;
And those sweet smiles upon his face
Are seals of God which angels trace.

XII.

THE WIDOW.

THE swiftest streams run soonest dry,
Though chafing with their shore ;
And heaviest showers that rend the sky
Are always quickest o'er.

All sorrow finds its sympathy,
And grief its counterpart,
However great the sorrow be,
Or broken be the heart.

The wing of death its shadow cast
Across the Wayside Inn ;
And solemn silence reigned, at last,
Where mirth so long had been.

The yonkers ceased their rollicking,
And held with awe their breath ;

They stopped the dance, they ceased to sing,
 When in the door came Death.

Van Horn, the keeper of the inn,
 The mighty drinker, died ;
With whom good Rip a guest had been,
 And jolly friend beside.

This drew him from himself, to feel
 For others' grief, and show
That sympathy was made to heal
 The wounds of others' woe.

The heart quick feels another's grief
 When wounded by its own,
And better knows to give relief
 Than else it could have known.

Rip closed the eyes of Hans Van Horn ;
 And to the mourners gave
Such tender words as one forlorn
 Could give beside the grave.

Remembering what the angel said,
 To stay his murmuring cries,
He praised the virtues of the dead,
 And pointed to the skies.

The dead man's widow, Anneke,
  Grieved more, the more he spake,
And sobbing loud she begged that he
  Would keep on, for her sake.

Then gliding from the willow-tree,
  All drooping in her charms,
The sorrow-stricken Anneke
  Fell swooning, in his arms.

Poor Rip was stifling with her weight,
  When they who stood around
The grave, with thought considerate,
  Laid her upon the ground.

Thence rising soon, they left the place,
  And closed the burial scene ;
And Rip went home with saddened face
  For Hans, and for Katrine.

THE WIDOW'S SYMPATHY.

The widow Van Horn was short and plump,
  And young and merry was she ;
And now, that her heart was wounded and sore,
  She needed much sympathy.

And this was the reason, from time to time,
    She sought the presence of Rip,
To sip the pity that trickled down,
    In honey-drops, from his lip.

And well she knew, in her own distress,
    To feel for the woe of another,
And therefore oftener sighed for poor Rip,
    As sister may sigh for a brother.

Her eyes were dark blue, but grew quite red
    By weeping alone all night,
But her dark-brown ringlets always looked neat,
    Whenever they came to light.

And very particular with her dress,
    As young widows ought to be,
No matter how terrible their distress,
    Was the plump widow, Anneke.

She knew that one use of the eyes is to draw
    The tears from the well of the heart ;
And never had widow a sprightlier tongue
    Her feelings in words to impart.

And therefore she oftener sought for poor Rip
    To cheer him with tears and tongue,

For she thought to mope so, and hang his head,
  Was pity for one so young.

She laughed in a week to her great surprise,
  While trying poor Rip to beguile,
By telling some jolly stories and jokes,
  To cause the poor fellow to smile.

The writers on human nature own up
  When trying to understand
Young widows, like Anneke, and confess,
  They yield to the subject in hand.

'T was therefore she oftener sought for poor Rip,
  That he might study her out,
And not be so stupid, but open his eyes
  To see what she was about.

STRATEGY.

She therefore, with strategic art,
  Pumped streams of pity up,
And poured it sweetened from her heart
  Like honey from a cup.

For she could feel for Bigham's state!
  Oh! she could sympathize

With one whose heart had lost its mate,
  Whose half was in the skies,

And only half was left below,
  To writhe and bleed alone,
In solitude with grief and woe!
  And all life's pleasure gone.

The words were wet, that crossed her lip,
  With tears, — for oh! her mate
(The same as with poor widowed Rip)
  Had left her desolate.

But she had noticed how the tree,
  When it had cast its fruit,
And lost its leaves, would, *seemingly,*
  Be dead from top to root.

And oh! how lone and sad it seems,
  Through winter's snow and rain,
Till warmed by Spring's embracing beams,
  It smiles and blooms again.

And so the widowed heart of man
  Is often sick of life,
Until he follows Nature's plan,
  And takes another wife!

8

And she had seen the rose-bush shed
   Great tears, as if it cried,
Because a favorite rose was dead, —
   As if *all* flowers had died.

But soon the bush would bud and bloom,
   And other roses bear,
And drown in beauty all the gloom
   It once was forced to wear.

'T was thus the heart that once has loved,
   And felt the widowed pain,
By love and grief has doubly proved
   Its power to love again !

And why should people born to make
   Each other happy here, —
To live and love for others' sake,
   And dry the falling tear,

To make the sunbeams dance around
   Each other's lonely heart, —
What right, or reason could be found
   Why they should live apart?

Her words like dripping honey fell,
   But Bigham's ears were dull ;
Therefore she sang, her love to tell,
   This song in accents full.

THE WIDOW'S SONG.

THE plant that bears a fragrant flower
    When nursed by sun and rain,
Though stricken by the tempest's power,
    Will bloom and bear again.

The flower may droop, the stem may bleed,
    When stricken by the storm ;
But still the plant retains its seed,
    Another flower to form.

Thus human hearts, though torn by grief,
    And widowed by the fates,
May bloom again, and find relief,
    By wooing other mates !

'T is not in love to droop and die,
    For love immortal is.
Though changeful as a zephyr's sigh,
    And frail as mortal bliss.

But 't is the nature of true love
    To blossom like a tree,
And bring forth fruit, and thus to prove
    Its immortality.

When last year's fruit is gathered in,
   Or fallen to the ground,
It surely cannot be a sin
   If other fruit be found.

They who have loved will love again, —
   Love is no barren tree ;
Whoever dies love will remain,
   And live immortally.

The heart will live, and love will bloom,
   That widows may rejoice ;
Nor will the *first* rise from the tomb
   To mar the *second* choice.

The first young mate may seem the best,
   Too good for earth by far,
And fly away, to find its nest,
   In some bright, distant star.

The first sweet rose, that blooms to cheer
   And beautify our homes,
Seems like the best that can appear,
   Until the second comes.

Then cheer up, widows ! cheer up, men !
   Nor chide the gloomy fates ;
Your drooping hearts will bloom again,
   And twine round other mates !

SHE said she never liked to sing this song
Since Hans's death, it seemed so *personal.*
To sing at all seemed, somehow, almost wrong ;
And yet she thought 't was philosophical,
And true to Nature, as a song should be, —
Especially where it treats of plants, and trees,
And flowers, and all that sort of things ;
For poetry should be like honey-bees,
Without of course their ugly little stings,
And gather sweets from every tree and flower,
In garden, grove, and buckwheat-field, and bower.

VAN BIGHAM felt her sympathy ;
 Their tears had mingled much of late ;
And who can tell but this may be
 A sign of mingling of their fate ?

But Rip's fond heart was far away,
 And buried in a distant tomb ;
And he had dreams by night and day,
 Which did not cheer the widow's gloom.

A vision of Katrina's wraith
 Had warned him thrice by day and night,
To keep inviolate their faith,
 And not a second troth to plight.

She seemed a holy bridal-queen,
  With crown of jewels on her head;
And yet she was the same Katrine,
  And seemed the living, not the dead.

The same sweet eyes that filled with tears,
  When they last parted, on the ship;
The same sweet face, with all the fears
  That trembled on her loving lip;

The same fair hand that clasped his own;
  The brow heroic when they parted,
Trying to hide, what yet was known,
  That she was almost broken-hearted;

Appeared before him, twice by night,
  And once by day; to him alone;
And warned him not to break their plight,
  With loving voice, nor chiding tone.

" I am your wife! No other one
  Can love, and long, and wait like me!
Now wait for me, as I have done, —
  As I have loved, and longed for thee! "

Sweeter the nights than brightest days,
  That held this vision to his sight;
He sought the dream, and shunned the rays
  That drowned such beauty in their light.

Thus lived the love in Bigham's heart,
    As lives the flower within its stem ;
And nightly tears, like dew, would start
    To crown it with a diadem.

Such manly tears did Bigham weep
    For one so worthy of his tears ;
And faithful image did he keep
    Of her, for all the coming years.

For they had loved each other long,
    With all their heart, in fatherland ;
Mingled their sorrows and their song,
    And walked together, hand in hand,

From early childhood, all the way,
    Till in the church he clasped his wife ;
Then left her, on that bridal-day,
    With all his world wrapped in her life.

And all his world seemed lost, we know,
    And all his life a desert wide ;
For deep as joy must sink the woe
    That fills its place, when joy has died.

BUT " Art is long " the poet said,
    And sweet is woman's tongue ;

And sprightly widows love to wed
　　Exceedingly when young.

And Van Horn's widow, Anneke,
　　Was young and sprightly still;
And had a tongue wherewith could she
　　Talk sweet, with wondrous skill.

And she was patient; Rip was kind,
　　And had a plastic heart;
And she had eyes; and Rip was blind
　　To widow-craft and art.

Three weeks passed on; and still she wept,
　　And needed sympathy;
And smiles and tears on hand she kept,
　　And used them witchingly.

She talked of other's slighted love,
　　As if it were her own;
And told how soon the mated dove
　　Would die if left alone!

She often sang mad Æfje's song, —
　　The Maid of Rockland Lake, —
Whose lover, Bertram, young and strong,
　　Had died for Æfje's sake.

Their tale she told, with widow-skill,
 To unsuspecting Rip,
To warn him not to craze, or kill
 True love, with cruel lip.

THE MAID OF ROCKLAND LAKE.

WHERE Rockland's peaceful waters lie,
 Upon their granite bed,
There lived a maid, in months gone by,
 Who now is with the dead.

And better be among the dead
 If what I sing be true —
Of heart made bleak, and reason fled,
 With love's long, last adieu.

Last winter, on a dreary night,
 Swayed by its boisterous breath,
I saw her, in the moon's cold light,
 Pale as the cheek of death.

The north wind whistled drear and chill,
 And she was thinly clad ;
Yet wandered she o'er vale and hill,
 And sang in accents sad.

Her song was of her lover dead ;
　And wild the vows she gave,
That she would constant prove, and wed
　Her Bertram, in the grave.

And oft she knelt upon the snow,
　And moaned a plaintive prayer ;
Mingled with broken sobs of woe,
　And laughter of despair.

Æfje was once most wondrous fair,
　They told me so who knew ;
Dark as the night her flowing hair,
　Her eyes a heavenly blue,

Her perfect form, with carriage meek,
　Moved with a sylph-like grace ;
The rose-leaf blushed upon her cheek,
　And heaven shone in her face.

Like Him, whose work of doing good
　Was constant day and night,
She gave unto the hungry food,
　To sorrowing hearts delight.

Her lover was a gentle youth,
　But he was very poor ;

And so her father's anger, sooth,
  It drove him from his door.

It drove him from his door away,
  Though he was good and brave;
He went, but ere another day,
  Had found a watery grave.

Oh bitter tears the maiden shed
  When forced from him to part;
And when they told her he was dead
  They say it broke her heart.

The night I saw this maiden fair,
  So lovely once, and sweet,
Her cheek was pale, and white her hair
  As snow-fall at her feet.

They tried to keep her safe at home,
  But oft she broke away,
Among the snow-clad hills to roam,
  Where her poor Bertram lay.

Her father wept, but wept in vain,
  For she was crazed and wild;
Nor could his tears, though poured like rain,
  Restore his only child.

" O Christ!" he cried, full oft and sore,
  In agonizing prayer,
" Pity my sorrow and restore
  My daughter from despair!"

In sooth it was a piteous sight,
  That aged man and gray,
Bowed down with sorrow every night,
  Lamenting day by day.

Could tears restore the word unsaid,
  That broke her heart in twain,
Could prayers restore to life the dead,
  His had not been in vain.

But ah! repentance came too late,
  Too late that father's prayer;
He'd driven a good man from his gate,
  His daughter to despair.

That night she came to Bertram's grave,
  And falling on the mound,
She called to him, the good and brave,
  There pillowed in the ground;

Then brushed the snow-shroud from the earth,
  With her white, trembling hand,

And laughed with strange and startling mirth,
    As, gathering up the sand,

She pressed it to her heart. " Oh why,"
    She moaned, " dear father, say !
Should Bertram, my own Bertram, die?
    Why keep him thus away ? "

Then suddenly, with strange, fixed stare,
    She cried, " Ah Bertram, dear ! "
(And wildly clasped the empty air,)
    " I knew I 'd find thee here !

" Now sit thee down and I will sing
    The song thou lovest so well ; "
Then sang, while at her feet, poor thing,
    The freezing tear-drops fell :

" Though cruel fate divide us here,
    And from each other far we 're driven ;
Yet this sweet thought our hearts shall cheer,
    We 'll meet again in heaven.

" Though our bright hopes must fade away,
    As rainbow's mingling tints are riven,
They yet shall span our stormy sky,
    And always blend in heaven.

" Though here they drive us from our love,
    And pluck our oft-watched star of even,
They cannot rend our hearts above,
    For all is love in heaven."

POOR Rip was moved ; and, like a chip
    Upon a rapid stream
Was borne along ; alas, poor Rip !
    And did as passive seem.

For, " Art is long " the poet said,
    And so is woman's tongue ;
And buxom widows love to wed,
    And will, if they are young.

And Van Horn's widow, Anneke,
    Was young, and had a will ;
A tongue and two bright eyes had she,
    And used them with much skill.

A widow brings, with woman's art,
    Experience to aid ;
And therefore acts more skillful part,
    And far outstrips a maid.

A month had passed, and still she wept,
    And needed sympathy ;

And smiles and tears on hand she kept,
   And used them wondrously.

She knew her time, she knew the man,
   And knew her witching power ;
And patiently held to her plan,
   And waited for her hour.

Then sweet words, from her rosy lips,
   She poured in rapid streams ;
Enough to drown a score of Rips,
   And twice a score of dreams.

For warning dreams and visions now
   Rip little thought, or felt ;
The coldness vanished from his brow ;
   His heart began to melt.

The widow's smile he caught, poor man !
   And then, somehow, her hand
Came also, without art, or plan,
   And was a magic wand.

He held her hand ; the widow's tears,
   Like gentle dew-drops, fell ;
She told her love, she told her fears ;
   But more I cannot tell.

Rip said he thought he ought to wait,
    At least, a little while,
Before he chose another mate, —
    But paused when she did smile.

She set the wedding-day before
    Bewildered Rip could think,
Then vanished, gliding through the door,
    And blushing like a pink.

———————

THAT night Rip dreamed the widow was a witch,
Riding upon a broomstick through the air.
Averse at first, he soon felt sudden itch
To be astride the broomstick, with her there ;
And in an instant found him at her side,
And flying with her through the yielding air ;
Himself a bridegroom, she the happy bride,
Riding to church, in good old fatherland ; —
The very church where he and his Katrine,
With plighted troth, had stood with hand in hand :
And then by rapid changing in the scene,
As dreams do change and give us no surprise,
The widow vanished, and his own Katrine
Stood there beside him with her downcast eyes,
And held her trembling hand in his, and said
The precious words that made her his for life ;

Then waked from joy to weep that she was dead,
And vowed he would not have another wife.

" I do believe this widow is a witch ! "
Said Rip, awake and talking to himself : —
" Or, I am like a blind man in a ditch :
Poor Hans is scarcely laid upon the shelf
Ere she turns round and wants to marry me ;
Tells me that Hans, her husband, was a sot ;
And that she feels her need of sympathy ;
And that she sympathizes with my lot,
For life is lonesome when one lives alone ;
And that 's the reason why so oft she comes
To cheer me, with her whining, wheedling tone ;
And says, It is the sunlight cheers men's homes.
What does she mean by sunlight ? Well I know
The sun went out when my Katrina died,
And left my home in darkness, me in woe, —
Left all the world in darkness, though I tried,
As man should try, to see supernal light
To walk by when the earthly failed my sight.
And yet a pine-knot, when the sun goes out
Can light a darkened room and make it bright, —
Enough, at least, to help one grope about,
And not sit moping with his silent grief,
Which, like a nightmare, presses out his life :
And mine half stifles me, till for relief
I almost cry aloud for my dead wife.

9

" What if I take this widow — marry her —
As she has willed I shall : what shall I gain ?
Not sunlight ; but the noisy, busy whirr
Of work ; and that, perchance, may drown my
    pain.
Not sunbeams, but the pine-knot's fickle light,
To take their place, — *her place*, alack the
    night !
This one to that is rushlight to the sun ;
But then I need the rushlight in the dark !
I cannot tell what web the fates have spun,
Nor how great fire may kindle from this spark ;
The widow seems to pity my distress ;
She smiles and sings ; and that is very kind,
Here in the lonely woods and wilderness ;
For somehow since Katrina's death I mind
Much more the dreary lonesomeness than when
She was alive : for then she came to me,
While I was musing in the woody glen ;
Or I passed to her far across the sea,
And talked to her, in fancy, half the day ;
And dreamed of her the sweetest dreams, by
    night.
But she has passed, and dreams have passed
    away ;
And her dear vision in the robes of white,
Which seldom has of late appeared to me,
This too will cease, and I shall be alone :

The widow, then, is a necessity !
Besides, she will not leave her work undone :
She has so willed that she and I shall wed.
This was her purpose when at first she heard —
So have I learned — that my Katrine was dead :
And well I know the saying must be true, —
If you don't court a widow, she'll court you ;
And if she does, the man must be a dunce
Who tries to fly, and does not yield at once.
But then I 'll tell her, like an honest man,
I do not love her, and I never can."

Next day Rip told her, as he vowed he would.
He said he 'd keep his promise, — marry her, —
But knew he did not love her as he should.
    Then she : — "'T is not that I would marry,
       sir !
For I have oft and often thought and said,
One husband is enough for one poor life.
And, long before good Hans Van Horn was dead,
I promised truly, as a faithful wife,
I ne'er again would marry if he died.
And so you see, if I should marry now,
Poor Hans will think that I have falsified,
And broke a solemn sort of marriage vow.
But then Van Horn, — he was so fond of gin,
And died so young, and drank and scolded so !
It would n't be so very much a sin
To marry you ! and yet I do not know."

The widow, pausing, with a gentle sigh
Looked down upon the floor, and seemed to wait
For Rip to comfort her with kind reply.
But Rip was wary now of widow-bait,
And merely said, 't was *pity Hans should die!*
   But Anneke still acted out her part,
With woman's tact, and willful, gentle art,
With widow's past experience to aid,
By which a widow far outstrips a maid!
With smiles and tears, she carried out her plan,
And Rip Van Bigham was a married man
Before he knew it! caught and held and bound!
Himself and cattle, cabin, farming-ground,
Woods, meadows, furniture, and household things,—
All by enchantment seemed to have taken wings,
And fallen, at the widow's charmed commands,
Down from Katrina's to the widow's hands;
To keep, to hold, to use, employ, and own
What was to be Katrine's, and hers alone.
   But yet Rip honestly confessed and said
" His heart was still Katrine's, though she was
       dead.
Man loves his first wife, if he truly loves,
As he can love no other in this life.
Their hearts are mated, like a pair of doves;
So have I loved Katrina, my first wife,
Who from my heart by death was rudely torn;
So can I *not* love you, do what I can, —
Not even you, the widow of Van Horn."

" Good ! " said the widow. " Rip, you are a
    man !
I love you better than I did Van Horn.
A fiddlestick for nonsense ! I 'll be good,
And fill Katrina's place as best I may ;
And do whatever she, if living, would
To make you happy, Rip, by night or day.
Men love their first wives, and, 't is sometimes
    said,
Admire their second. If you do that much
For me, and not forget your first is dead,
Why, love or not : 't is all the same in Dutch,
At least to start with ; so let 's go ahead,
And let Love follow after, if he will ;
And if he wont, why, let us both keep still,
And shame the little rascal for his sloth :
What 's fair for one is surely fair for both.
I promise you I 'll be, love or no love,
As good a wife as you a husband prove ;
By which I mean I 'll be the best of wives,
And you the best of husbands, all our lives."
    And then she fixed their wedding-day. at noon
That day a week. " She needed but a day ;
Her wedding-dress was ready : and she soon
Could change her mourning garbs for dresses gay.
She 'd dyed a couple, when Van Horn first died,
For company and Sundays, — that was all ;
And these, of course, she now would lay aside,

And not go covered with a funeral pall.
She meant to act like any other bride,
And take her bridegroom with becoming pride."
   Rip thought, at first, the widow spake in sport;
But, when he found her serious, humbly said,
" He thought the time she set was rather short;
Out of respect and honor for the dead,
The day should be at least six months ahead."
But she, in gentlest mood, at once replied, —
" Concerning Hans, I think 't is hardly so:
I knew he 'd die *six months* before he died;
Which makes a world of difference, you know,
The same as if he 'd died *seven months ago !*

" And then Katrina had been dead some time
Before the news could reach you o'er the sea;
And that came months ago; so what 's the crime
Of being at once what we intend to be ?
The dead are dead, and we 're alive and free.

" You know what Hans was ; and I really think
I was his widow while I was his wife ;
For he was often drunk, *dead-drunk* with drink,
For months before it burned away his life :
Poor Hans and Death had such a tedious strife !

" I 'm glad, good Rip, that you do not like gin !
You used to take with Hans a little flip,

Like other yonkers, at the Wayside-Inn;
And I was glad to have you do it, Rip!
It did me good to see you sit and sip.

" But if you put fierce liquors to your lip,
And gulp them down, as Hans did in his dram,
And so get drunk like him, I 'll curse you, Rip,
As sure as I 'm the daughter of Van Dam ;
And you will find a woman's curse no sham.

" Hans saw not in his cups the lurking death !
The coiling serpent hid itself from sight,
Till by degrees it poisoned all his breath,
Then struck him with its deadly fang that night,
And left him dying from its mortal bite.

" Poor man ! and yet he loved me so, he said,
As he had always loved me from the first.
I 'm sorry to speak evil of the dead ;
But, like the quenchless fire of the accurst,
Was Hans's burning, everlasting thirst.

" Hans said he did n't think it was a sin
For one to drink when dry ; and he was dry
As soon as he had drunk, then drank again
The liquid demons of old Holland gin !
And I could only just sit down and cry,
And almost long yet fear to see him die.

"He died a victim to the cursed tank,
And drank up every thing on earth he had.
His farm, his tavern, horses, — all, he drank;
My household things! O Rip! that was too bad!
And left me here a widow, lone and sad.

"I tell you, Rip! that was a day of woe,
And just as fresh as though 't were yesterday,
Although he died more than a month ago.
And now, dear Rip, I wish to hear you say
You 'll not drink gin in any shape or way.

"Before we 're married, *just this noon a week,*
Declare you don't love gin, nor any thing
That makes such horrid blotches on the cheek,
And swells the nose, and carries in its sting
Poison that kills the beggar and the king.

"I do not like to be a widow, Rip!
So promise me you will not drink, like Hans,
And kill yourself, and so give me the slip.
I know you wont, but say so in the bans:
A widow here has such a slender chance!"

  Rip felt he was a straw upon the stream,
To float which way the widow might decide;
And he had learned that 't was no idle dream
That, when a widow wills to be a bride
He who resists, resists both wind and tide:

Therefore replied, — " 'T was well as she had said,
Or what she might thereafter have to say ;
Only he felt, in honor for the dead,
'T was rather soon to fix their wedding-day :
But still 't was better she should have her way.

" He wished that Hans had lived a sober man,
And had not died at all, if that could be.
But Hans had carried out his mortal plan, —
Had had his way, and died.   And she, — why she
Must now have hers," said Rip, abstractedly.

" Hans has not only given me a wife
By doing as I urged him not to do,
But also an example for my life, —
A warning not to drink till I am blue ;
And I will mind, my dear, both him and you.

" I did not wonder Hans began to bloat
Before he 'd swallowed half his house and farm :
I saw his horses gallop down his throat,
And told him they would do a deal of harm,
By such a course ; but he felt no alarm.

" I then made up my mind to stop my flip,
In hopes that Hans would therefore stop his gin ;
And often went a-dry," said honest Rip,
" And choking for a drink, day out and in.
But my example was not worth a pin.

" Now he is dead and gone.　And my Katrine
Is dead and gone ! " he added with a sigh ;
" Death, like a black-robed priest, has come between
Our dead and us, to join us with the tie
That binds the living pair till one shall die.

" So be it, then ! we cannot stay the Fates ;
To-day a week send for the Dominie,
And let him tie the knot to make us mates.
I 've always held, what is is sure to be :
And this no doubt is down in the decree ! "

XIII.

THE DOMINIE.

THAT day a week, the Dominie appeared,
　　By message sent across the Tappan Zee :
Through watery dangers and far distance, cheered
　　By prospect of good time and wedding-fee,
　　He came, equipped with due authority.

He was a goodly man, of great renown
　　In all the country round, both far and near :
On either side the Hudson, up and down,
　　He much was loved, and held in reverent fear,
　　And spake such words as did men good to hear.

By free consent, endowed like feudal lord ;
  Withouten feudal fiefs or lands or power, —
Without the brazen trumpet and the sword,
  He ruled the land as doth the summer shower,
  That falls to bless the earth with fruit and
    flower.

" What says the Dominie to " this or that ?
  Decided questions, quarrels, and the like,
And knocked the stoutest controversy flat :
  It settled matters of the Church or pike,
  And stopped the tide of passion, or a dyke.

When mounted on his horse, or in his " chair," —
  A two-wheeled vehicle of ancient days, —
All knew him through the country, everywhere ;
  For none but he e'er rode in such a chaise ;
  And e'en his horse had ministerial ways.

When standing in the pulpit, — and he stood
  In many a one, for miles and miles around, —
He looked a symbol of the pure and good,
  If any such in all the world was found ;
  And preached the doctrines solid, clear, and
    sound.

When, calling on his way from house to house,
  His robust frame and cheery face was seen,

The sight was hailed with joy by men and vrouws;
  And little children came, with instinct keen,
  To climb his knees, and on his chair to lean.

Learned with the learned, he prattled like a child,
  And laughed as free as any water-brook,
When with the little ones ; so meek and mild,
  So much in sympathy, in heart and look,
  With man he was, though steeped in lore of
    book.

His buckled shoes ; his broad three-cornered-hat ;
  Knee-breeches, tight above the swelling hose ;
The easy way in which he always sat,
  And smoked his pipe with calm, serene repose, —
  Would in our day look oddly, I suppose.

In our fast times, the Dominie might be thought
  Long-winded, for he preached a full long hour,
And sometimes two, when Satan must be fought,
  Until the truth had triumphed o'er his power:
  Such wind would make our Gospel milk turn
    sour.

But in the days when people came from far,
  And walked ten miles to church, sometimes a
    score,
Bringing their lunch along, it was no bar

If they took back, beside the feast, in store
A basketful of Gospel crumbs, or more.

Things different seem from different points of view:
  We like short sermons, they liked sermons long;
They liked the old, we like to have things new;
  We like the doctrines weak, they liked them
    strong;
We believe, as they did, our religion true,
But then we wish as little as will do.

Hence they the church clock placed outside the
    tower,
  That all to church might always punctual be,
Nor lose a moment of the sacred hour:
  We place it *inside*, that the Dominie
  The time to let us out may promptly see.

The thorn in Dominie's flesh, not all concealed,
  And yet not fully known, was Dominie's wife.
It could not all be hid, and, half revealed,
  Distorted, grew to fierce domestic strife,
  By tongues that love to mar a good man's life.

But she was crazed. How well he bore her
    tongue,
  How meekly all her strange, erratic ways,
Remembering what she was when she was young, —

All this was known, at length, and turned to praise
    The slanderous words that stung his earlier days.

These things I tell not for her detriment,
    But for the sake of truthful history,
And for his name and fame who came and went
    Long years with this great grief, unmurmur-
        ingly, —
    The good, long-suffering, cheerful Dominie.

She took delight in thwarting all his plans ;
    Tore up his sermons ; sent his horse astray,
When harnessed for a journey; stopped the bans
    Of marriages ; appeared in strange array ;
    And teased the patient Dominie night and day.

On Sunday, when the church was going in,
    She locked him fast within his study-door ;
Then told inquiring wardens he had been
    Through Sleepy Hollow on the day before,
    Since when he'd nothing done but sleep and snore.

She knew by instinct, or by dream profound,
    In which she was the Dominie's equal mate,
His plans and projects, in parochial round ;
    And with his secret thoughts seemed intimate,
    By intromission strange and intricate.

To journey with him wheresoc'er he went,
　But most of all when he should go alone
For public weal, her mind was always bent :
　"I needs must go!" she said in wifely tone,
　"Because we twain are one in flesh and bone."

He often hid his horse and chair apart
　In distant orchard, or more distant wood,
Then slipped around when ready for a start,
　Unknown to her, he thought, when, lo! she
　　stood,
　All ready by the chaise, with shawl and hood !

When on the way, she 'd stop the pony short,
　And bid the Dominie out, to walk up hill ;
And, after he had reached the top, for sport
　Drive on, and make him run and walk, until
　'T would seem his flesh must surely take it ill.

In sooth it was a sorry sight to see
　Such weighty man up a high hill ascend ;
For large, though comely, was the Dominie :
　His weight of head did make his body bend,
　And breathe so short it did to wheezing tend.

The pony, once a kind, obedient horse,
　Began at length his cunning ears to drop
Backward, to catch the pro-and-con discourse ;

And then to loiter, then to halt and stop,
And by the road the wayside grass to crop, —

For he was injured much by their discourse.
    When one said, Go ! the other one said, Whoa !
Divided counsels first perplexed the horse,
    As they do yonkers in our homes, we know ;
    Then spoiled him, as they do the yonkers too.

The horse, by nature amiable and mild,
    And regular in his habits as a mill,
Though petted much like favorite, only child,
    Learned from his mistress, by example ill,
    To balk, and fight to have his way and will.

The Dominie preached a sermon from this text,
    To show how children learn to disobey.
By family conflicting councils vext,
    They, puzzled, know not which to choose ; so
        they
    Become self-willed, and balk, and have their
        way.

He set the pony up, for an example,
    Before the congregation, till they saw
With their own eyes the illustrative sample ;
    And all confessed his words were true as law,
    And must have hit the pony in the raw.

It did him good ; I speak to pony's praise !
　　Thereafter he did lead a better life
By straightening many of his crooked ways ;
　　And he and Dominie, when without his wife,
Did jog along without a jar of strife.

But, now that Bigham's wedding-day drew nigh,
　　He found her dressed from hat to shoes in
　　　　white ;
And sooth she was, to any mortal eye,
　　With face all chalked and corpse-like in the
　　　　light,
　　A ghostly, weird, and most sepulchral sight.

Her willful purpose Dominie tried to change, —
　　She must not go ; when, lo ! she thus began, —
Strange fire within her eye, her language strange :
　　" 'T is *you* had better change your purposed plan
　　Of marrying one who *is a married man !*

" I 've dreamed a dream ; and, Dominie, beware
　　How you attempt to cross the Tappan Zee !
The man you go to marry I could swear,
　　If that should be demanded, is not free
　　From his first wife, no more than you from me.

" I know his story, and I know his lie ! —
　　' He left a wife in Holland, and she died.'
10

That wife I saw last night.   She did not die !
  Her *wraith* came to me in my dreams, and
      sighed,
  And told me that the Captain's lips had lied.

" ' His lips, but not his heart,' she meekly said,
  ' Had brought the mortal lie across the sea.'
' But look ! ' she said ; ' I live ! I am not dead ! '
  And thus three times did she appear to me ;
  By which I know the dream 's reality.

" I laugh to think you fear lest I should plan
  To see this marriage ! If I go at all,
'T will be to stop it with a corpse's ban !
  I 'll be a wraith, and take the funeral pall
  To catch the widow-bride in, if she fall.

" I will not go ! I do not choose to go !
  I 'll be no party to this woeful fun, —
This widow throwing off her weeds of woe,
  Ere yet her husband 's cold, for this new one ;
  This widower with a living wife undone ! "

The Dominie was glad to be released,
  But felt the shadow of prophetic fears,
Which fall upon the greatest and the least ;
  Besides, he knew his wife, these many years,
  Had other dreams than those which fancy rears.

But soon his journey drove the dream away,
　While in his mind he thought Rip's history o'er:
And he had known the Captain many a day;
　And all seemed clearer as he thought the more;
　And he passed on undoubting, as before.

Leaving his home, he left all care behind,
　Full sure 't would not take wings, but wait him
　　there;
And shadows fled before his sunny mind,
　While conning o'er, in brisk and wintry air,
　His marriage ceremony quaint and rare.

At length arrived, he found the two together, —
　Van Bigham and Van Horn. The day was
　　cold,
But not too cold, Rip said, for wintry weather;
　Just such a day as Cato, black and old
　And weather-wise, the night before foretold.

THE WEDDING.

No marriage-bells rang out their merry chimes,
　The frozen echoes of the woods to wake;
Nor liveried lackeys, in those sylvan times,
　Nor white-gloved grooms, nor frosted cards and
　　cake,
　Were needed for a decent wedding's sake.

The trees were dressed in purest snow-white robes;
    The sleigh-bells rattled out their roundelay;
Huge fires roared on the hearths, in burning
    globes,
    And shed a radiance like the sun in May,
    Which helped the widow blush and Rip look
    gay.

The guests came gathering in from far and near,
    Some riding horseback, pillion-saddle-wise, —
The trusty vrouw behind her goodman dear,
    But most in sleds, of various forms and size,
    For snow had fallen betimes from thoughtful
    skies.

When all had come, and when the time had come,
    The twain stood forth before two vacant chairs;
And all the guests, as if by tap of drum,
    Arose, dividing off in several pairs;
    And then the Dominie began, with prayers.

These done at last, he, rustling in his gown,
    With solemn form and long rehearsal told
How marriage pure from Eden had come down,
    With orange-blossoms wreathed and rings of
    gold,
    And strewed the earth with blessings mani-
    fold;

How great a blessing Eve to Adam was ;
   How Jacob toiled and toiled to get a wife ;
How the old patriarchs broke the marriage laws ;
   And bigamy brought family feuds and strife,
   And poisoned with its roots the springs of life.

Thus step by step, down to that present day,
   Stopping at Cana half an hour at least,
To see the water-pots, in long array,
   Pour forth their God-made wine to cheer the
      feast,
   And blush for man whom wine can change to
      beast.

Then joining, hand to hand, Rip and Van Horn,
   He bound them fast with clasps of solemn vows,
From which by death alone could they be torn ;
   Then bade the husband kiss the blushing spouse,
   In sign that love should ever rule their house.

THEN smoked the festive table with its food, —
   Game, venison, fowls, and crisp, infantile pork ;
While in the midst a drunken rooster stood,
   Ready to crow at touch of carver's fork.

Sweet cider, flip, hot rum, well spiced and strong,
   And, last and least, the home-made currant-wine,

Came, when the joyous feast was well along,
　　To free the tongue, and make the face to shine.

Then came the story, and the merry laugh,
　　That shook the rafters and the oaken floors,
And made the old man throw away his staff,
　　To mock the winter grumbling out of doors.

And then the dance, as hearty as the feast,
　　With foot as merry as the merriest tongue ;
And all must join, the greatest and the least :
　　None was too old to dance, and none too young.

Old Cato, known to all the neighborhood,
　　As black as Night, with eyes like twin half-
　　　　moons,
From his old fiddle of well-seasoned wood,
　　In measured time, scraped out the rustic tunes.

Thus passed the day until the sinking sun
　　Advised the guests 't was time to kiss the bride,
And leave her to the bridegroom she had won,
　　And homeward hasten on their evening ride.

Such was a wedding in the olden days,
　　When joy was pure, though rude and rustic born ;
And Rip was married in these simple ways,
　　And took to wife the widow of Van Horn,
　　And paid the Dominie's fee in oats and corn.

XIV.

WIFE NUMBER TWO.

Of all the strange things in this world of ours,
Not to name other worlds not so well known
    In the upper or lower division,
Beyond our inquisitorial powers, —
In this world, where so many things are strange,
As science and art have everywhere shewn,
    In questions for our decision,
Whatever the object that comes within range
    Of our inward or outward vision,
There's nothing more strange than the heart of
      man,
    Be it human, or be it inhuman,
Unless, by a chance, we happen to scan
    The stranger heart of a woman.
Search all the way down, from tallest to tall,
And all the way round, from greatest to small,
And on till you come to nothing at all,
You'll find, in all cases, the heart to be
A puzzle, a cheat, and a mystery.

Old Goldsmeller, dead in the churchyard now,
Who had such a narrow and puckery brow,
    And such a contracted breast,
And always spoke hollow and empty, somehow,
As if there was nothing at all in his chest, —

Though every one knew he had plenty of pelf,
But that he always kept all to himself;
Who never would smile, for the reason he feared
If he smiled, some prodigal thief might steal it,
And so at his private expense be cheered,
And he at some far future day might feel it.
  And the same with his bread and cheese;
In short, he acted so niggard a part
That nobody knew he had any heart
    Till he died of heart disease.

  And so with the widow of Hans Van Horn:
While yet she was merely the maid Van Dam,
Those rollicking blades whose hearts she had torn
All called her coquettish, an empty sham.
But, when they saw what a good, loving wife
She made Van Horn; how she helped him through
        life,
And grieved at his death; and felt for poor Rip, —
The very same rollicking, slanderous crew,
Although she had given them all the slip,
Were forced to confess, with a sober lip,
That, so far from having no heart, they knew
The plump little thing had enough for two!

  With this explanation, need I relate
How Rip soon learned to succumb to his fate?
He moved to his cabin; and there, between
Enlarging and fixing and change of scene,

He almost forgot to think of Katrine,
Except when the tree he 'd named for her name —
Which stood in the door-yard, looking the same
As when he planted it, tender and young —
Would seemingly speak to him with the tongue
Which sweet zephyrs gave it, softly and mild;
Or when, in the windy tempest and wild,
He heard it moan out with a human moan,
Poor Rip would then sometimes weep like a child,
    But he always wept alone.
And he wept alone for the reason why
A man never likes to be seen to cry;
And a happy bridegroom, he knew, ought to sing
On a natural key, and not on a flat.
But Rip had a genuine heart, for all that;
For the heart is a very strange thing.
    And Anneke led him a very good life;
She made the log-cabin look neat and clean,
And a tidier door-yard never was seen.
She did her best, with a smile on her face,
With busiest fingers and winning grace,
In every way, to fill up the place
Which she knew for all that, with instinct keen,
Still empty remained, of the dead Katrine;
For having the instinct of womankind,
She jealous became of the dead Katrine,
    Though not a word she said.
But Anneke had a feminine heart,

That needs to be sought, to be wooed and won,
And needs a whole husband, and not a part,
Though the very best under the sun.
But, think what she might, she managed her tongue
With womanly skill, and womanly tact ;
For well she knew she was handsome and young,
And, like a wise woman, made most of the fact
In her toilet and dress and every act,
And left the remainder to time.
Nor did she for evermore harp and chime
On the ancient affection of dead Van Horn,
To show how her heart had been rudely torn,
When, dying, he gave her a sudden slip,
And left her alone in the world with Rip :
Nor held up his virtues, that Rip might see
A model of what a husband should be,
As many a man, in the course of his life,
Perhaps may have heard from his second wife.

The widow Kissam, who married Verbeck,
As soon as the rules that held her in check
Would allow, at least it was so understood, —
For all the Nyackers said that she would,
And some of them said she married too soon, —
Had scarcely got through her new honeymoon,
And settled again, before she began
To hold up Kissam as the model man,
After the usual custom and plan.

And Verbeck, who every one thought before
As moral as any on Tappan shore, —
Who never was known to drink or to swear,
And never appeared to have any care
To fret him, or make him the worse for wear, —
Began to grow fretful and glum and old,
And looked like a grumbling, masculine scold,
And swore like a terrible trooper bold,
And guzzled hot gin like a spirit vext
That cared not a schnapp for this world or next.
And the more that he drank and scolded and
 swore,
His wife only held up Kissam the more ;
And the more that she held up Kissam, the more
Verbeck only grumbled and drank and swore,
And every day worse than the day before.
Thus she, like a wise, affectionate wife,
At any time ready to give her life
To save her husband the sullen Verbeck,
Was driving him down, without the least check,
To the place where no one would wish to dwell.

By making her first husband's name a bell, —
Her tongue for clapper, — Kissam rang the knell
Of her second, until, with stagger and swell,
He tumbled headlong into Hades, pell-mell ;
But whether he fared there nearly as well
As with her at home, I hardly need tell.

And there was Deacon Van Tassel, good **man**,
Who went to work on the usual plan
With his number two, the meek Betsey Ann,
Until, in a year, he had almost killed her
With his number one, dear Mary Matilda !
By boasting so much of his sainted first,
He filled the second with wrath, till she burst.
And, had it not been for the vent in her eye,
And a chance now and then to slip out and cry,
She said she believed in her heart she would die.
He gloried to tell Betsey Ann, his second,
How Mary Matilda, his first, had been reckoned
A pattern in every arrangement of life, —
Of course an obedient, model wife,
Avoiding all gossip and scandal and strife ;
That Mary Matilda did this and that,
Wore such and such dresses, and such a' hat,
And made her home pleasant with pious chat ;
That Mary Matilda was fond of dishes
That always agreed with her husband's wishes,
And so very prompt and nice with the food
'T was always in time, and always was good ;
That Mary Matilda took care of her feet,
And did not go gadding from street to street ;
That Mary Matilda took care of her tongue,
And did n't allow it to go as if hung,
Like that of a hollow brass bell, to be rung
Where'er the noisy thing chanced to be swung ;

That Mary Matilda was prompt at meeting,
And always noticed the poor with a greeting;
That Mary Matilda read very much
Her good old Bible, in vellum and Dutch;
That Mary Matilda was ever given
To duties of earth, and service of Heaven:
In short, the good Deacon, with no complaint
Of his second, made out his first such a saint,
That she, though trained in the shade of a stee-
    ple,
And fond from her girlhood of all good people, —
Though likewise she made no sort of complaint,
Yet heard so much of Matilda the saint,
As pattern of good and chider of evil,
Her love for the pious grew very faint,
And got so she finally hated a saint
As once she had hated the devil.

But, after a time, the Deacon began
To smell a rat, like a sensible man, —
The grave-rat, gnawing by night and day,
And eating the heart of his wife away:
The Deacon, in other words, found it best
To leave his Mary Matilda at rest,
Like a saint as she was, in Abraham's breast,
And not keep bringing her back to his own,
Where now Betsey Ann had such rights alone.

From that time onward, the Deacon began
To appear to his wife like another man.
And Mary Matilda, where she should be,

In mansions of bliss, soon got herself free
Of all those features which gave Betsey Ann
A fit of hysterics or sulks, to scan ;
And made her, instead of praying for grace,
Desire to go, when she died, to the place
Where *she* would n't see the *sainted one's face.*

When left to herself, from that very day
She tripped about in her natural way,
And bloomed and blushed like a flower in May ;
And seemed much more of a saint than a sinner
When the Deacon sat down to his daily dinner,
Without the old skeleton, or the least
Of Mary Matilda dear, at the feast.
From that day forth, there was no more strife
In the Deacon's house through the Deacon's long
    life :
And sweet Betsey Ann was as good a wife
As Mary Matilda had ever been ;
And the Deacon well knew and felt it within,
Though number one, of course, was the *first,*
And *best* of course, if the best or the worst.

Without confession of any transgression
'Gainst rhyme or reason in this one digression,
Lest others may ask for the same confession,
" I return," as the Dominie used to say
When owning that he 'd been out of the way, —
As Dominies sometimes do in our day,
To fetch back the sheep who have gone astray,

By telling a story some truth to enforce, —
" I return to the thread of my long discourse,"
Though I hardly know where to look for the
      thread,
In such a snarl of the living and dead, —
Such tangled-up mixtures of bit and shred,
Like Dominie's sermon, whose parts he meant
Should somehow lean to the general bent
Of the end that he had in his wise intent ;
Though, as for the ending, nobody knew
If the Dominie had any end in view !
Admitting he had, and allowing he knew it,
He travelled so far in coming round to it,
They thought, who waited to see him quite through
      it,
'T was so far ahead he never could view it.
His " Finally " never was able to do it,
Though often sent forth as if to pursue it,
Like a hawk on the track of a frightened bird ;
But still his *Finally* was the good word
That awakened the church in every part,
And started a smile from every heart,
As if a fresh plant of some heavenly grace
Had suddenly sprouted in every face.
But " Finally," though 't was able to send
Such thrills as to make the church sleepers bend,
And those who had ears all their ears to lend,
As doubtless the Dominie did intend ;
Yet " Finally " was not always the end.

'T was merely used for a little delay,
To help the Dominie feel for his way
When, as I have said, he had gone astray,
And think what 't was he was going to say,
And catch the thread of his straying discourse ;
As salt is made use of to catch a horse.
So now, with a final to " Finally,"
For which you will thank the good Dominie,
" I return to the thread," and find it to be
In Bigham's log-cabin on Tappan Zee,
In the hands of industrious Anneke,
In the eye of a needle, which needle she
Is plying just now perseveringly,
In making a cushion of silk and leather.
The work seems to fret and puzzle her much ;
For often she stops, and mutters, in Dutch,
That what she is sewing she 's doubtful whether
Was ever intended to come together !
The pieces are puzzles, in shape of hearts,
Of zig-zag patterns, uneven in parts ;
And Anneke stamps her foot as she plies
The needle and thread, and nervously tries
To sew them together, and make them fit.
Now, pausing, she laughs at her lack of wit, —
With one breath saying ' she 's nearer to it ; '
With another, ' she knows she 's not gained a bit : '
Then, speaking aloud to herself alone,
Says, " That's the way with Rip's heart and my
          own !

For Rip will have a dead queen on his throne;
Though dead and long buried, beyond the main,
Katrina must sit in his heart and reign!
He acts just as crazy as crazy Jean,—
The love-cracked widow of Philip of Spain,
Who bore the corpse of her husband, they said,
Wherever she travelled, from place to place,
Refusing to own that the king was dead;
Now kissing his lips and patting his face,
Then breathing the love of a living wife
In the ears of a corpse, as if it had life!
And Rip acts the same with his dead Katrine,—
As silly and crazy as crazy Jean!
He carries her image from place to place,
And thinks of her always, I know by his face;
Though he tries to hide his thoughts from my
          sight,
He calls out her name in his sleep at night!"

Thus Anneke talked to herself alone,
Still plying away at the work undone,
With fast-running tongue, till Bigham came in,
When, ceasing her humble-bee sort of din,
She rose to salute him with smile and kiss,
In sign of her perfect connubial bliss;
Which shows the old time was very like this.

Good Rip, with dog Rover and gun, had been
In neighboring woods, for a pouch of game;
And Anneke vowed she never had seen

11

Him look so well since the day he first came
To Tappan Zee, in the old *Pioneer*,
Though every day he was growing more dear;
And, casting her sweetest smile in his face,
And taking his gun with a winning grace,
And laying it up in its usual place
On the hickory hooks of a beam overhead,
As one might have put an infant to bed,
Then, taking his pouch of partridge and quail,
And praising the marksman that could not fail,
And patting dog Rover, who wagged his tail
And put out his paw, as if with intent
To acknowledge the flattering compliment,
She acted a scene of life every day:
For Anneke acted, as one might say,
The happy wife in a natural way.

 The worm at her liver, of course, she knew;
As well as the Spartan boy in the story
Knew the fox was tearing his insides out, —
A test of his pluck decidedly gory,
And proof that *theft* may *be covered with glory.*

 Fierce jealousy gnawed at her heart, 't is true;
But, holding it in with a courage stout,
She gave it no loop-hole of word or pout
By which to escape to her husband's ears,
And never allowed him to see the tears
Which over and over again she shed
Because his heart was the throne of the dead,

Instead of the living wife he had wed ;
For wisely she thought, by holding its breath,
To smother the green-eyed monster to death.

COMPANY.

THE day had come round for their " company ; "
That is, for friends and acquaintances near
To come, in their turn of neighborly cheer,
And take a warm, sociable cup of tea, —
A Dutch custom held by their children dear.
And *Tea* meant coffee and cider and beer,
Roast turkey and goose, broiled chicken and
      game,
Some cold, and some smoking hot from the flame,
Hot muffins and short-cake, waffles and sweets,
To mix with or follow the savory meats ;
And olekokes, krullers, and such boiled cake ;
With mince-pies and custards close in their wake ;
And, hindmost of all, the jellies and jam ;
And all things real, and never a sham,
From welcomes at first to the last good-by !
They parted without a drop in their eye,
Or waste of sweetness in kisses and sighs,
Or one of our modern Frenchified lies.
    Such, whilom, the social gathering
Which white-haired Winter was certain to bring

From house to house, in the friendly old time,
To keep the heart warm in the icy clime,
What time he began to drive, blustering, round,
Or came on swift runners with muffled sound ;
Or sat at his loom in the snow-lined cloud,
On lengthening nights, to weave a white shroud
To cover the stiffened and stark cold ground ;
When plow, field, and farm were weather-bound,
And held in the rigid grasp of his hands
As stiff as if grappled by iron bands ;
And farmers were kept, by his stern commands,
From daring to touch a field of their lands.
They met in this way, and conspired together
To laugh in the face of his threatening weather ;
And, casting the shadows of care behind,
They jingled bells in the teeth of the wind,
And mocked the old blower with joke and song
While cantering, trotting, and gliding along.
And now they were gliding with merry sound,
And jingling their bells, o'er smooth, snowy ground,
To give Rip his turn in the festive round.

And Rip and fair Anneke, hand in hand,
Were getting ready the fat of the land ;
That she the good lady, and he the lord,
Might honor their guests at the festive board ;
And Cæsar, unctuous and shiny as fat,
And ready at work whate'er he was at,
For master or mistress, in doors or out,

As strong as a crowbar, nimble and stout,
And happy as nimble, went whistling about,
Preparing for quadruped-guests a stall,
And shelter and beds and supper for all.

The sun had been in the sulks the whole day,
Because of some storm-clouds crossing his way,
And sullenly kept himself out of sight ;
And went to bed early that afternoon,
With scarcely a smile as he sank to rest
On his regal couch in the purple west,
And saying aloud to himself, " I 'm blest
If Rip and the earth dont take it to-night ! "

But Cæsar predicted an evening bright,
Because, as he said, " the light of the moon
And stars on the snow would make it as light
As daylight, unless it should storm quite soon."
This said while plucking the feathery game,
And shining before the bright kitchen-flame,
Where Mistress Anneke frequently came
Without the least blush, or a sense of shame !
For time had not come for a lady to boast
She did n't know beans from butter and toast,
Nor a bit of a broil from a piece of roast,
Nor a chicken well dressed from a chicken's ghost.
The time was n't yet for accomplished spouse
To know just nothing about keeping house ;
When mammas, to make their daughters complete,
As Nature intended, for man's helpmeet,

Must dress them like dolls from their head to feet,
And teach them the art of simpering sweet,
And how to preserve their dear hands from soiling.
   In those vulgar days, the men had to eat,
And women to help them by sometimes broiling,
And sometimes roasting and stewing and boiling;
Nor was it an honor to shirk from toiling,
Nor shameful to keep the dinner from spoiling.
In short, in those days, the best sort of spouse
Was one who always looked well to her house
And husband and children, that kind of thing;
Who knew as well how to work as to sing,
Could tell a sheep's leg from a woodcock's wing,
And never was *finished* until she knew
Roast-beef from a regular family stew.

   And dumpy, fair Anneke, in those days
Of piping hot suppers and tea and dinner,
   And all things in that connection,
Stood foremost of all in the neighbors' praise;
And barring her tongue was sometimes a sinner,
   Was almost up to perfection.
And well the dexterous Anneke knew
The gastric gate of the savory art
Stands close at the head of the avenue
That leads from the stomach up to the heart! —
That she who her husband's love would retain,
And she who her husband's lost love would gain,
To keep forever in sunshine or rain,

Be he a saint or sinner,
May try as she may, and will try in vain,
  If *she neglect his dinner.*
And half the family quarrels that come,
To drive a regular man from his home,
  On Discord's jarring wheels, —
As well as dyspepsia and heart-disease,
Free-love, and that kind of affinities,
And cheap divorce any time you may please,
And similar evils that shock or tease, —
  Come from irregular meals,
Not always the fault of the scolded cooks.
And half of the sour words that are said,
And more than one half of all sour looks,
  Proceed from sour bread.

  But Anneke's bread was sweet, not sour ;
And Anneke's meals were true to the hour ;
And Anneke therefore wielded a power
  That reached to her husband's heart !
She, little by little, began to trace
Her way to that most desirable place
By aid of the above-mentioned gastric grace,
And nature in constant bloom on her face,
  And also the aid of art.
And so, when the " company " came together
That stinging and biting mid-winter weather,
Of course not to sting and to bite their neighbors, —

For visitors never do that, —
While they were all talking of plans and labors,
  In regular tea-drinking chat,
In the old-fashioned way that they used to do it
In forefathers' days, on old Tappan Zee,
Fair Anneke dropped in each cup of tea
A mixture or charm, when nobody knew it,
Which acts like a touch of the blarney-stone !
And presently every one's tongue began,
With honey-bee hum, in the blarniest tone,
To speak in the praise of fair Anneke.
One after another they raced and ran
  For words to convey their pleasure
That Anneke had so noble a man,
  And Rip had so great a treasure ! —
That never was cottage or house more neat ;
And never was housewife looking more sweet ;
And never had company better treat ;
And never was tenderer, juicier meat ;
Nor better-baked biscuit, from whiter wheat ;
Nor any thing else, than they had to eat,
(Then took a little more tea.)
And never did fire-place give better heat,
To warm the whole body, from head to feet,
Wherever one happened to place his seat :
There could n't be built a jollier fire ;
The back-logs and fore-sticks, and all between,
Were piled, — they could n't be piled any higher.

A cheerfuller fire they never had seen,
   And never expected to see!
And thus they continued, as they began,
   Still harping on Anneke;
Till, blushing, she whispered to Rip, good man,
To stop those folks, or they'd praise her to death.
But still their tongues blarnily raced and ran
As long as they had a remnant of breath,
   Then took " a little more tea,"
And on again, with a galloping sound;
So that, when the apples and nuts came round,
The apples and nuts were additional ground
   For praising sweet Anneke!

Then Rip began to think he'd found
A pearl on old Tappan Zee
(For pearls in the ancient Zee abound)
   Which he had failed to prize,
And that his friends knew more its worth
   Than he; for they were wise.
So well the tongues of festive mirth
Had harped and sung — the precious dears —
To praise the jewel he had on earth,
   He thought not of the skies.
And so, from opening first his ears,
   He opened now his eyes;
And Anneke ne'er had looked so fair,
So like a costly jewel rare,

In her good husband's charmed sight,
As when the sleigh-bells on the air
Rang out and died, at twelve that night.
    And thus it was that " company "
    And Anneke's gentle art,
And regular dinners, time, and tea,
    Healed Rip Van Bigham's heart.
And Anneke found, when Spring came round
And snow had left the frozen ground
    With Winter's dismal weather,
The puzzle which she oft had tried,
With thread and needle plied and plied,
And stamped her foot and groaned and sighed,
And sometimes swore, and often cried,
    At last was sewn together!

XV.

REVIVAL.

TIME, like an eagle with young on her wing,
Comes flying, and bearing her fledgling, Spring;
And drops her, amid the sunshine and damp,
On southern slopes of a forest-fringed swamp;
Thence, chirping, and hopping from bog to bog,
Though sometimes half frozen with cold and fog,
But still growing stronger from day to day,
By little and little she feels her way,

By following the sunbeams, till she is found
On green sheltered spots of the upland ground.
Thence, skipping from place to place around,
But timidly, wary, and slow at first,
She comes where the crocus begins to burst
From soft, lowly graves, and snowy, white shroud,
Like Lazarus at the voice of his God.
We soon find the welcome prints of her feet
Where soft-breathing meadows and forests meet;
Then still higher up, among fields of wheat;
And away among nooks of emerald green,
Where Winter, half melted with heat, is seen
Repairing his broken chariot-wheels,
And scowling at Spring for chasing his heels;
And where the old tyrant will come again,
With forces of drizzle and sleet and rain,
To fight for the mastery of the clime,
And bind the timorous Spring for a time.
But she, still smiling, though half in tears,
With sunbeams armed the fight will renew,
And with her myriad emerald spears
Will riddle his white-mailed armor through,
And chase his fierce, blustering allies off:
Then all his morsels of cold will be spent;
And then the old tyrant his crown must doff,
And his robes, in the fervid firmament.

Now Sparkle Creek throws off his chain,
　And laughs and trips away
Like boy long held by books or rain
　Let loose for a holiday.

And now and then a pioneer bird
　Comes, like a spy, alone ;
Then flies away with joyous word
　That winter months have gone.

The blue-birds seek the hollow stump,
　And find their last year's nest ;
And Phoebe-birds come, with a jump,
　From their long winter's rest.

The little chippy hops around,
　Without a bit of fear,
Where'er a seed or crumb is found,
　Just as he did last year.

Children, with faces all aglow,
　Bring wild-flowers from the wood :
They 've heard the robins ! and they know
　That Spring has come for good !

A SONG OF SPRING.

THEN sing all men, and take a part,
    With happy hearts and voices ;
Let none be silent while the heart
    Of Nature so rejoices.

Let grateful lips find joyous words !
    For all the air is ringing
With joyous songs of happy birds,
    And happy streamlets singing.

The Earth, now rid of Winter's crew,
    And torn from his embraces,
Is spreading out her carpet new
    For wood-nymphs and the Graces.

The Spring goes forth, though coy and shy
    And blushing like a maiden,
To offer incense to the sky,
    With flowers and leaflets laden.

The shivering forests, stripped and bare,
    Through all the winter sighing,
That stood so stark in the icy air,
    And groaned like mortals dying, —

Appear again in mantles bright,
    Flung o'er their shrivelled features,
And stretch their arms to catch the light,
    Feeling like new-born creatures.

Murmuring their thanks, the rustling trees
    Put on their green spring dresses;
While zephyrs kiss the laughing leaves
    With tenderest caresses.

The bees have left their empty hive
    To work among the daisies;
Glad for the chance to work and thrive,
    They hum their grateful praises.

The spring-peeps, in their swampy home,
    Prophetic pipe their voices;
Foretelling plenteous time to come:
    And the farmer's heart rejoices.

The plough-boy sings, across the fields,
    Driving old Buck and Berry;
Their hardy necks the oxen yield,
    Patient as he is merry.

The sower sows, and soon the seeds,
    Into a harvest growing,
Will teach him that all human deeds
    Are but the seeds we 're sowing.

And seeds long buried now arise,
  A resurrection vernal;
As man shall rise, though first he dies,
  To live a life eternal.

Then sing all men, and take a part,
  With happy hearts and voices;
Let none be silent while the heart
  Of Nature so rejoices.

Rip joined the universal song,
Glad that the Spring had come again,
With flowers and music in her train;
And thanks to Him, to whom belong
All thanks, he gave, as good men should.
His barns were full, his oxen strong,
His wood-house filled with seasoning wood;
His cows and sheep rejoiced with young;
And as he drove his team afield
His heart made music with his tongue,
Hoping for what the ground could yield.
For Love has dreams, and Hope has eyes;
And when he saw the flowers arise,
And grain, long buried in the earth,
From womb of graves with glorious birth,
His thoughts flew upward to the skies,

And backward far across the sea,
And forward to the glad surprise
Of life from death, foretold to be,
When his sweet flower should leave its tomb,
And in immortal beauty bloom.
Though happier now than he had been
Since Death first robbed him of Katrine,
Yet her dear face oft comes between
Him and the bustling Anneke;
And fancy paints what she shall be
When blooming in eternity.
Go where he may, do what he will,
Her gentle face is with him still.
She draws him to the cherry-tree,
Not now to weep there, but to sing
As he beholds its blossoming,
And thinks of the eternal Spring;
For love and hope look far away
Beyond the night to find the day;
Beyond the winter of the tomb
They look for Spring when Spring shall come
Arrayed in everlasting bloom.
Nor is it strange that thoughts like these
Should float before Van Bigham's eyes,
'Mid fresh-born flowers and new-robed trees,
Which teach us that the dead shall rise;
Nor that the evening twilight hours
Should find him sitting, musingly,

Beneath Katrina's cherry-tree,
Now blossoming with bridal flowers,
As she was dressed that long-passed day,
Like these, alas! to fade away.
Beside, 'twas time to hear once more
From fatherland's too distant shore.
We long to hear, what yet we dread, —
The last words of the loved and dead.
, Rip longed to hear those words from her.
Long months had passed since the *Rollicker*
Had left Manhattan Isle, to trace
Her path o'er Ocean's wrinkled face;
And now 'twas time for her return,
For which he looked from day to day,
With fever of the heart, to learn
What prayers were on her dying breath,
And mournful items of her death,
Till then kept back by strange delay.
This brought her image back again,
In thoughts by day, in dreams by night;
But more in pleasure than in pain,
And less in darkness than in light.

A VISION.

WHILE musing thus, one twilight hour,
Beneath her blooming cherry-tree,

A chaise with two passed hurriedly.
Was it a dream, or fancy's power,
That brought her image to his eye ?
Was that Katrine?   It could not be:
It was ; and yet it was not she.
Her gentle look, that same sweet face,
Made up of every heavenly grace ! —
But she was dead : and Ocean's wave
Stretched far between him and her grave.
And yet that vision flitting by, —
If she had dropped down from the sky,
And stood before him, eye to eye,
She had not looked more like Katrine
Than that sweet face he just had seen !

The chaise had passed, — he sat alone !
But not that face and form were gone.
He seemed to be in some bright dream,
Floating again down Life's swift stream,
With all his early hopes and fears,
With all his love and joys and tears.
He saw Van Dam, he heard his voice —
Brave Captain of the *Rollicker* —
Bidding him calmly to rejoice ;
For he had news to *tell of her !*

He heard no more : but when he woke
There stood Van Dam as when he spoke
The words that brought the sudden night.

Was it then *not* a dream of light?
There was his friend, whom he had seen
Within the chaise, with his Katrine, —
Kind Captain of the *Rollicker*, —
And he had heard him speak of *her*.

Could it be real? had he seen
His dead, his own beloved Katrine?
He closed his eyes; — how strange was this!
Could this be his immortal bliss?
Had time thus borne him on its wing,
So soon, to the Eternal Spring?
But no! there stood his friend, Van Dam,
With those old words, " Good Rip, be calm! "
He saw his face, he heard his voice,
That bade him calmly to rejoice,
For he had done his errand now!

What was that beaming on his brow?
Was it a halo circling there?
Did he a crown of glory wear?
The unreal did the real seem,
If 't were a dream, or not a dream.
The words seemed floating from Van Dam,
Who stood with glory round his brow, —
"*Good Rip! I 've done my errand now!*
I 've brought her! but, good Rip, be calm!
Good Rip, I 've brought the dead to life!
She lives! and you shall see your wife."

Then silence came ; and clouds, once more,
And then the vision as before ;
And then the face of Anneke,
With wonder and perplexity.
He would be calm, and held his breath,
To think if this were life, or death ;
A dream, a vision of delight,
Or fairies, working spells, by night.

It was no dream.   Van Dam was there,
Beside him in the evening air ;
And with him anxious Anneke,
Beneath Katrina's cherry-tree.
He listened to his voice again,
As if it were an angel strain :
" Good Rip ! I have a yarn to spin
When you have strength to hear it, friend,
From the beginning to the end.
Katrine is at the village inn !
I find 't is kept by Buckhout now,
And Anneke, my niece, the vrouw
Of poor Van Horn, is spliced, somehow,
To — well, I know it all, old boy !
So take my hand ! I wish you joy ! "

He waited ; but Rip answered not ;
Bewildered, dumb, chained to the spot,
With blank amazement stupefied,

He merely moved his lips and sighed ;
Then seemed to think he had replied.

Van Dam still held him by the hand.
" Stand up ! " he said, " we 'll soon see land !
Come, shipmate ! courage ! be a man !
Are you in heaven, or in Tappan ? "
" In heaven," said Rip, " if I have seen
The blessed face of my Katrine !
She passed here, and I saw her face ;
And you were with her in the chaise."
" All right, good Rip, the very thing !
You see, I lost my reckoning,
Not knowing these land soundings well.
I was to hail you first, and tell
My yarn, before you saw her face,
And set you trim, with stay and brace.
All right, now ! Come, if you are steady ;
Katrine is crank, but brave and ready ;
If you 're as staunch as she, you 'll weather
This little storm, with ease, together."

Doubting if things were what they seemed,
Awake and yet afraid he dreamed, —
For Rip had dreamed like this before,
Only his dreams gave no surprise,
That she long dead should live once more,
And act and move before his eyes, —

Half stunned, and half unconscious, he
Followed Van Dam mechanically ;
Like dreamer walking in his sleep,
Who safely treads some giddy steep,
Where one false step, or hasty breath,
Might plunge him to the gulf of death.

They met, gazed in each other's face
And in each other's arms were grasped,
In one, long, breathless love-embrace ;
Their very souls together clasped.
The twain were one ; — heart grown to heart,
Flesh grown to flesh, and bone to bone ;
Each of the other vital part,
Two beings swallowed up in one.
They did not speak, they could not speak ;
And good Van Dam stood silent by,
Stout sailor as he was, as weak
As they, — a child with tearful eye,
And quivering lip, and sobbing sigh, —
While Rip received his dead to life ;
And she, his patient, faithful wife,
Received, that hour, reward for years
Of painful waiting, wracking fears.
Their swelling hearts have scarcely power
For joys that crowd in that brief hour ;
And dumb with ecstacy, they seem
Entranced with love like them that dream.

THE CAPTAIN'S YARN.

" You see they thought Katrine was dead,
And signalled, with the winding-sheet,
From Barthold's house-top, as they said
They would while off and on I beat,
That morning, waiting for the sign;
And so, instead of fetching your Katrine,
I had to bring the news, that broke
Your heart, with every word I spoke.
But, Rip! you see she did not die;
Or if she did she came to life
Again, because she was your wife;
And no one told a willing lie,
Save Death himself, who played the sham.
In my next trip to Amsterdam
They told me how they 'd been deceived,
And thought her dead while yet she lived.
She almost made that voyage.   Tossed
For a time upon the unknown sea,
Her brave, good bark, at length, had crossed,
And made for port.   But just as she
Was casting anchor, suddenly
Her sails were struck aback, and bore
Her homeward, to her native shore.
I hailed her heartily; and I said,
' Is this Katrine whom I left dead?'

And then I told her how her death
Had stunned you, took away your breath.
Poor thing! I should n't have told her that!
It liked to 've killed her, knocked her flat;
As if a squall had struck her square,
And swamped her; with me standing there;
Me, — Captain of the *Rollicker!*
Feeling as if I 'd murdered her.
She righted soon; and then Barthold,
Her father, spun his yarn, and told
How they had thought her dead, and made
Her shroud, at last; and even laid
Her out.   But there their hands were stayed.
They saw her coming back from heaven;
And then they knew she had been given,
A second time, to them and you.
Then how they wished you only knew
That she had risen from the dead!
But ships were coming in, instead
Of leaving, when they wished to send
The hurried word, by mail, or friend;
And when a chance had come, alack!
The war with England drove it back;
And from the sea the swift-winged word
Flew homeward, like a frightened bird,
And went to roost, with long delay,
Till month on month had passed away;
Though every moment seemed a day.

At length the *Rollicker* appeared, —
A ship, good Rip, that never feared
An Englishman, nor Neptune's gale,
Nor any craft that carries sail.
You know, good Rip, what she can do !
Well, with Katrine, and twenty more,
Safe-housed aboard, she fairly flew
Across the waves, from shore to shore !
Nine knots an hour were in her wake,
(I think for your Katrina's sake ;)
And the whole voyage was merely sport.
And here we are, all hands in port ;
With news and letters, and Katrine
As safe and hearty as a queen ! "

The Captain's yarn was not more strange than true,
As Barthold's letters showed, in tracing through
From first to last, the sickness of Katrine, —
Her seeming death, and her recovery,
And what in seeming death her eyes had seen,
And ears had heard, in that far land between
Our world and the immortal world on high.
At first, when Rip had parted from her side,
Tearing himself away from his young bride,
While yet the orange-blossoms wreathed her brow,
She watched, with hope, his ship's receding prow.
But when the fame of the great storm came in,
With wild reports of wrecks, that had not been,

Fear chafed her anxious heart by night and day,
Till weakened, she became an easy prey
To slow, consuming fever, which remained,
Smouldering within, in spite of healing art,
That cannot reach the fever of the heart.
Thus wasting while twelve moons had waxed and
          waned,
With hope deferred, they closed her curtained eyes,
Supposing she had passed into the skies,
Just at the time Rip's messenger had come, —
Good Rip Van Dam — to bear her to his home.
But strange to say, and oh! how glad to say,
That night of death had turned to life's sweet day!
And then did Barthold's trembling pen relate
The mystery, which none can understand,
Before they pass beyond death's narrow gate;
What she had seen in that strange border-land,
'Twixt earth and heaven : he wrote with pious hand.

THE TRANCE.

WHILE thus in seeming death, she dreamed a
          dream;
     Or passed (she knew not which) the gates of time;
And crossed a narrow, dark repulsive stream;
     Then saw, at once, a most resplendent clime,
Unvexed by human groans, unstained by sin or
          crime.

High up she saw a city, on a mount,
　　Too glorious to behold with mortal eyes ;
And by its lower gate a golden fount
　　Of liquid pearls, — the tears brought to the skies
From broken hearts that wept for sin, with mourn-
　　　　ful cries.

Beside the gate she stood, and saw bright troops
　　Of happy spirits coming from the earth, —
The care-worn pilgrims, changed to joyous groups,
　　Rejoicing more than in their day of birth,
Who made the air resound with songs of holy mirth.

From that high place the earth was but a speck ;
　　And all this life a short and troubled dream ;
Its plans and schemes were but a worthless
　　　　wreck, —
　　A child's lost ship upon a little stream, —
So small did this great world unto her vision seem.

She waited for her turn to pass within
　　The golden gate, that breathed forth sweet
　　　　perfume,
Too glad she had escaped the world of sin ;
　　And glad for others, who from darker gloom
Passed by her to receive their life's immortal bloom.

She saw them come from sickness, pain, and
　　　　death ;

From lonely solitudes of homes bereaved ;
From tortured beds where pangs were in each
    breath ;
  From hopes deferred which early shrouds had
    weaved ;
And from low graves, where they in vain had
    moaned and grieved.

The tired pilgrim, burdened with his load ;
  The war-scarred soldier, fresh from battles won ;
As on they toiled up the ascending road ;
  The racer who triumphantly had run ;
And faithful servants who their Master's work had
    done.

And many a child she saw by angels borne, —
  Their little faces all with joy aglow, —
Which, just before, the pangs of death had worn ;
  While at their empty cradles far below,
The mothers' broken hearts were bleeding with their
    woe.

As back and forth the angels ever flew,
  With crowns of light, on swift and fragrant
    wings,
And saints the golden gates were passing through,
  She saw the seats where joy immortal sings,
And caught the breath of flowers which youth un-
    dying brings.

And yet she stood while others entered there;
   When lo! a voice, like music of a bird,
Said, " Go, my child! Go back to earth and
     care!
Go; do; and speak the gentle act and word;
To show the sorrowing ones what you have seen
     and heard."

Then she awoke. From heaven to earth she
   came;
   Transformed anew, and tried as gold is tried; —
Our sweet Katrine; the same, yet not the same,
   As on that Sabbath night we thought she died,
Triumphant in the risen, glorious Crucified.

She brought to earth the fragrance of the skies;
   White rose-leaves, fresh from heaven, were on
     her cheek;
A sweet soft light shone in her loving eyes;
   And when she spake, in accents low and meek,
His name, we thought we heard an angel speak.

From her fair brow the glory had effaced
   Of pain and sorrow every furrowed line;
And none but angel-fingers could have traced
   Those lineaments of love and peace divine,
With which her gentle face, henceforth, will ever
     shine.

She told, by slow degrees, the strange event ;
   And bade us put the shroud and mourning by ;
For back to earth her spirit had been sent ;
   And she should live she knew, and should not
      die,
For well she knew such heavenly vision could not
      lie.

Her strength came back. And Hope, with joy-
      ous wing,
   Flew, like a bird, to nestle in her breast,
And all day long prophetic notes did sing,
   To soothe her heart and make it truly blest,
And did, with gentle wing, fan her to healing rest.

As Mozart's daughter sang his soul to heaven,
   Love sang her heart away to that far land,
Where her twin-heart with poverty had striven
   To build their home ; for there she saw him stand,
And beckon her to come, with joyous, outstretched
      hand.

For him the voice, in her ecstatic trance,
   Had bid her soul return to earth again,
To help him bear its toil, and seeming chance,
   Its burdens, and its cares, its ills and pain,
Who for her sake had toiled, and should not toil in
      vain.

New-born to us, — a gift the second time, —
    She grew in strength, and with a soul as pure
As if it had not left the better clime,
    Again to sin, to suffer, and endure,
Which in our mortal state of all things are most
      sure.

As birds grow restless with increasing strength,
    And feathering out too large for their old nest,
Stretch forth their wings and fly away, at length,
    So she now longs to fly and be at rest
On Hudson's bank, on her beloved husband's breast.

Receive her as a gift the second time
    From Heaven and us; as we ourselves received
Our twice-born daughter from the holy clime;
    And may your heart, at last from woe relieved,
Rejoice with joy more than with sorrow it has
      grieved.

XVI.

A SNARL.

THE grab-game of Fortune is funny enough;
But rather unequal, and sometimes rough,
In this little, tumbled-up world of ours.
A few catch most of her golden showers,
And have a deal more than they ought to wish,
Of wife, or of widows, and widow's dowers,

And surfeit on many a dainty dish;
While many get merely a kick and cuff,
And find the whole grab-game terribly tough, —
A scuffle and scrabble for worthless stuff.
E'en so it was, in this case, with good Rip : —
When women were scarce and in great demand,
As sometimes they are in a new-settled land,
Dame Fortune gave many a fellow the slip,
Which comes in " betwixt the cup and the lip,"
And sent him a jogging along through life
Without the supporting prop of a wife;
While Rip, lucky man! was husband to two.
And this at a time of general want,
At least when wives were provokingly scant,
Because the country was new.
The rollicking yonkers all thought it too bad,
Though some of them laughed as if they were glad,
That Bigham had more than he wished he had;
Like him with the elephant.
Poor Rip was perplexed, and he scarcely knew
What under the heavens, on earth to do.
Supposing one wife for a man enough,
He feared that his course might be rather rough
By undertaking for two.
He tried to guess out this puzzle of fate,
His heart in a fever, his brain half turned;
But the more he studied the less he learned;
Till, finding 't would take a much stronger pate
Than his to decide what course he should take,

He sent for the Dominie.
He begged him, at once, " for dear mercy's sake,"
To come *alone*, at as rapid a rate
As in his power the journey to make,
From Tarrytown over the Zee ;
For he felt uneasy, inside and out ;
In fact, hardly knew what he was about.
Drawn hither and thither, this way and that ;
Loving Katrine, and afraid of a spat
Whenever he showed it ; for Anneke
Had vowed she 'd have no partiality.
And gentle Katrina was meek and mild ;
As good as could be, but almost as wild
At the strange events, and the stranger state
In which she had found her affairs of late.
He, married to one as much as the other,
Much feared he 'd go mad with the puzzling bother
Like the ass between the two bundles of hay,
In equilibrium, standing at bay,
Unable to move a foot either way,
And puzzled to know what to do or say.
And so he relied on the Dominie
To come if he would, and kindly advise
Whatever the course of duty might be.
He wished to see with the Dominie's eyes,
The way that was right, and proper, and wise.

The Dominie came, as a Dominie would,
Whose mind was intent on offices good ;

And barely was seated, when Anneke
Made him a glorious cup of tea,
With lunch of sweet-smelling savory food.
She looked like a full-blooming rose forlorn,
When dreadfully done for, and almost torn
Away from its stem ; and hanging her head,
With fresh pendant tears, she modestly said,
She felt she was in the place of the dead,
And lying alone in a churchyard bed,
Much more than she felt like a wife just wed.
'T was he who had tied, and he must untie
The marriage knot, if he thought it best ;
But she would be hanged ! — she meant, she 'd be
        blest,
If she would n't much rather die !
For what would the gossiping yonkers say ?
And how they would crow, especially they
Whom she had provoked by giving the slip,
And jilted them all by marrying Rip !
" You know," said she, " how the slanderous crew
Got the plaguy story afloat, somehow,
That I charmed Rip's cider, and made him blue,
Then bound him with the connubial vow,
Before he got sober ; which is not true.
And who would consent to marry me now,
If known to have been unmarried by you ;
With not a dollar of dower in view,
And neither a maid, a widow, or vrouw ! "

Thus Anneke seized on the Dominie's heart
By her tea and tears and feminine art,
And muddled, perhaps, the good man's head.
Or, it may be, the Dominie was afraid
Of his crazy wife, who appearing to know
His errand again, had tauntingly said :
" *Ah, Dominie! did n't I tell you so ?*
You know I did, sir ! Aha, sir ! oh ho !
I tried to stop you from going ; but no !
Off, sir, you would go, and marry the beauties,
As if you thought it the choicest of duties
To cross on the ice-drifts o'er Tappan Zee,
And wade through snow to your horse's knee ;
But *I* told you plainly how it would be ;
And now I 'm glad that you went, for you see
That I only told you of what I knew ;
For what 's a dream good for if 't is n't true ? "

The Dominie slipt away from the shrew,
Her words still hallooing, " Husband ; you know,
And don't you deny it ! *I told you so !* "

For these, or some other reasons like these ;
Or, maybe, the Dominie wished to please
All parties, and so with all sides agree, —
With Rip, with Katrine, and with Anneke, —
He gave an answer which each of the three
Might make whatever they wished it to be.
The chroniclers state, without derision,

The words of the Dominie's wise decision, —
" *Rip, taking the whole of your case in view, —*
If ever man lived for whom it would do
To live with two wives, the man, sir, is you! "

An oracle never, with words more wise,
Bestowed on the questioner more surprise
Than these which came forth from the smoking shrine
Of the Dominie's theological mine ;
And never was mortal less satisfied
To whom a wise oracle had replied.

" And as to your marrying Anneke,"
Explained the astute, smoking Dominie,
" 'T was done of course unintentionally,
Before Katrina, your first wife, was dead,
And therefore to both you 're rightfully wed.
Such cases as yours must always be rare ;
But *some of the patriarchs had a pair,*
And Isaac's and Jacob's were not more fair
Than Rip's ; and though they brought trouble and
        care,
And though 't was in the original plan
That *one* wife should be enough for a man ;
(And so I have found it most truly to be
In my own case," sighed the good Dominie ;)
" Yet as we now live, in some sort, the way
As patriarchs did in their ancient day, —
With people so few, and our country new, —

If ever man lived for whom it would do
To live with two wives, the man, Rip, is you;
Since you are rightfully married to two."

The old common law had n't much to say,
But winked a good deal, in our fathers' day;
And hence when the Dominie went his way
He knew that Rip would not be molested,
But live on quite happy, and unarrested,
With twofold share of connubial bliss
To comfort his home in the wilderness.
But other folk's homes, like other folk's hearts,
Are quite covered o'er; and little we know
Of all that is passing within, — what smarts,
What achings, what battles, and wounds, and woe

XVII.

THE HAUNTED HOUSE.

OUR shadows will follow where'er we roam.
Rip sought to escape low spirits, at home,
By flying to those of the Wayside Inn.
His cabin was haunted! Such wizard din
Was never yet heard since Satan and Sin
Their progeny foul, of accursed birth,
Let loose to harass and to vex the earth!
The goblins and imps were everywhere;
Ghosts wandered around the cabin at night,
Strange noises were heard in the misty air,

Supposed to be witches on broomsticks there ;
And men, who were gifted with second sight,
Saw enough to chill the doughtiest soul
That ever yet laughed at a ghost or ghoul.
In our more civilized, busier day,
When the din of life keeps witches at bay,
We scarce can conceive of their fearful sway,
In the olden time, when they had their way.

At first Rip thought that the yonkers, at nights,
Were helping the witches. Such sounds and sights,
Such tricks with the cattle, horses, and sheep,
And harness, and ploughs, while he was asleep ;
Such cackling of fowls, and flying of geese, —
Then always the signs of a coming breeze, —
Such wars of the bees, in the fields of clover ;
The bars let down 'twixt the pasture and corn ;
Such fighting of cocks, and growling of Rover,
As soon as the night gave place to the morn ;
And jolly old Cæsar's ebony face, —
Always a symbol of African grace,
And smiling with joy in every place, —
Now turning from plastic flesh into flint ;
And even his eyes beginning to squint,
    By looking two ways at once ;
So that from being a merry, smart fellow,
    Poor Cæsar became a dunce ;
And from a jet-black turned black mixed with yel-
        low,

And ripened too fast, and grew very mellow,
By too much of village inn,
And smelt like a mixture of negro and gin;
And even the scarecrow, ragged and torn,
Would come from its place, in the field of corn,
Each evening, and peer through the window-pane
But always was found at 'ts post next morn,
As sentinel, guarding the sprouting grain,
And stood there till evening set in again;
When stalking across the soft furrowed ground,
Again at the cabin window was found.

Not even the household waters ran smooth,
On which sailed the tongue of fair Anneke,
Though Rip did as much as he could to soothe,
By pouring oil on the rough, troubled sea,
The angry waters would contrary run,
And battered away the old fallacy,
That " two heads are better than one."
And Rip discovered, half crazy and wroth,
And hungry from sun to sun,
His dinner half raw, or else overdone,
That " too many cooks spoil the broth."
The meal-hours jumbled, like the meal itself,
Were very uncertain, and came pell-mell;
And if a cold rasher were left on the shelf,
It vanished, — but how, nobody could tell;
So that, in a world of breadstuffs and meat,
Poor Rip was hungry, with nothing to eat.

The friend of his leisure, his faithful loom,
The gift of his father, from fatherland,
Had covered its face with a web of gloom;
And palsied and still was its busy hand;
And brooding it sat, all haggard and mangled,
Like victim escaped from robbers, half strangled.
The warp-threads and woof, though perfectly right,
When left to themselves for repose, at night,
Next morning were sure to be snarled and tangled.

And so with Katrina's good spinning-wheel,
And distaff and yarn, and old-fashioned reel;
However they worked, with orderly care,
When under the eye of their mistress fair,
If she turned away, in a moment spare,
For walk in the garden, to take the air,
They turned the whole room to a witch's lair.
Indeed the whole house had passed through a
          change,
And every thing in it was weird and strange;
For the very kittens had ceased to play,
And changed their kitten-like features,
And looked like infantile tigers at bay,
Or dwarfed old grimalkins, scarred and gray;
And growled, and quarrelled, and battled all day;
And hissed out and swore what they had to say,
In a caterwauling, blasphemous way,
Like terrible rampant creatures.

SOLACING SPIRITS.

AT length Van Bigham was driven away,
By the wicked goblins and ghosts and witches,
To seek for solace 'mong spirits more gay,
Who sing and seem happy even in ditches.
Bewildered he was, and twisted awry,
And now and then had a drop in his eye,
And tried to walk with his feet to the sky,
So great was his distraction.
Old Cæsar, his man, on such an occasion,
Persuaded good Rip, who needed persuasion,
To not go home to the cabin that night,
But sleep at the village inn.
And Cæsar chuckled to show his delight,
And danced with satisfaction,
Because his kind master nodded his head,
In sign that he wished to be put to bed.

PERHAPS it was a venial sin
For sleepy man, as Rip had been
Through weary weeks of home-made din,
To try a few small naps,
After his tavern-tea and schnapps,
In Buckhout's cosy bed.
He felt confused about the head,
His eyelids pressed his eyes like lead,

And Cæsar scarce the word had said
Ere he was fast asleep.
His breathing now was free and deep,
Like one shut off from care and trouble,
To whom the world is but a bubble,
He hardly snored, but slept and slept,
I know not for how long a time ;
But midnight hours had softly crept,
And muffled men had stalked on crime,
And many a sick-bed friend had wept,
And looked on death, in every clime ;
When suddenly loud shrieks and cries
Arose, and roused the village inn,
Like groans of a dying wretch, who dies
With an unforgiven sin.

At once the guests sprang out of bed,
And ran, with Buckhout at their head,
To trace the groans, and bloody deed
From which such groans might well proceed.
A wizard sight they saw; alack !
Poor Rip Van Bigham on his back ;
His brow stone-cold, his pale cheeks wet,
And trailed by cold and clammy sweat ;
His fingers clutched, like eagles' claws ;
His mouth wide open with fixed jaws ;
His eye-balls glared with vacant stare,
And stood on end his bristling hair ;

In short, like statue of Despair,
And still and motionless as dead,
Was Rip, recumbent in the bed.

    They shook him; and he howled a howl,
Like shrieking of a wounded ghoul!
He looked about with frightened stare,
His eyes like eyes of lobsters stuck out;
And getting sense, he cried, " O Buckhout!
I 've had a terrible nightmare,
Or something worse, I cannot tell;
It seemed that all the imps from hell
Had come and tried to pull my pluck out.
They first played leap-frog on my breast!
Jumped up and down! staved in my chest;
Then thrust their hands, and felt about,
And seized my pluck to pull it out;
The moment that you came and woke me,
Their grinning chief, meanwhile, to joke me,
Was asking how *they did at home;*
And how *I'd like with him to come,*
To hear the everlasting gong?
And said, if I should want more tongue,
He 'd send me one up from below, —
A forty-horse-power tongue to go;
But if I could, upon the whole,
Get on alone with my good fight,
Why, then he 'd take my *pluck to-night,*
And call again to get my *soul.*"

Then jolly old Buckhout laughed outright,
At Rip's queer dream and ludicrous plight;
Till cramping, he laid on the floor to roll.
But Rip looked solemn, as well he might;
For how could he comprehend
The nightmare's warning, and hideous sight,
Of demons that gave him such a fright!
Or what such awful dream might portend,
Of Satan claiming to be his friend?
Or where such a joke might end?
And this made Buckhout only laugh more
To look at Rip's solemn, sober face;
And then the bystanders following pace,
The tavern was soon in a wild uproar,
And splitting its sides with laughter;
Which the imps, from rooms and halls a score,
Threw up from cellar to rafter.

To Rip, still nervous, the men looked grim,
Undressed, and holding their candles dim;
For seeing things yet through wizard film,
What now he saw and what in his dream
Were so mixed up, in the mist and din,
That goblins and men of the village inn
Seemed like the mingling waves of a stream,
On the edge of a tumbling cataract.
And goblins and men and devils grim
Seemed all to have joined to laugh at him,
So much was his mind distract.

And though awake the rest of the night,
The grinning goblins were still in sight,
And danced and tortured him with affright,
Till morning drove them off with its light;
And then he felt, what he knew before,
That *tavern spirits torture one more*
Than the very worst spirits at home.
He found that witches could go and come,
Not one of them could he leave behind,
No more than if 't were part of his mind;
For every goblin, nightmare, and elf
Seemed, like his thoughts, a part of himself,
And knew his secretest heart's intent,
And followed him wheresoe'er he went.
Rip therefore pronounced the way to the inn
A dangerous road to travel;
That the imps that revelled in flip and gin,
And joined in the roystering, tavern din,
And leered from the bowl with sinister grin,
And laughed at honest men's care and sin,
Were not the best friends to help him unravel
The tangle and snarl he was in.
And though they drowned his troubles awhile,
'T was done in such Beelzebub style
As added to their fuel;
Which showed their cunning and goblin guile.
The way they pulled at his pluck, when asleep,
And danced on his chest, with laugh and leap,

Was not much less than cruel.
And then their promise to *come again,*
To lay his domestic care and pain,
And every family squall,
Because his name was upon their roll;
And that they *would call again for his soul,*
He did not like it at all.

But still he found, wherever he went,
The goblins followed, on evil bent;
Like him who travelled to fly from care,
But found it close to him everywhere, —
In foreign lands, at sea, in the air, —
Wherever Rip went the imps went after,
With taunting jibes, and half-smothered laughter.
At home or away, in doors or out,
Like dogs that follow their master about;
Alone in the fields, on hill-side or meadow,
They stuck to his heels as close as his shadow.
" Aha ! " they whispered among the trees,
Where they were brewing a midnight breeze,
" Aha ! here comes the man with two wives !
How happy he looks ; and how he thrives !
If ever man lived for whom 't would do
To marry two wives, and live with two,
Why Rip 's the man ! how merry he is !
With double cups of connubial bliss,
And double rows of connubial jars,

Brimful of jams and family sweets ;
And all things pleasant, except the wars
Uxorious, which the goodman meets !
Aha ! if e'er, in any land,
Was found a man with strength to stand
A pair of wives at his command,
Why, here 's the very case at hand !
The keen-edged Anneke and Katrine,
A pair of shears, and he between ;
A jollier mortal ne'er was seen
Since jolly days of patriarchs !
His wives !   Oh won't they leave their marks
On husband's face ; and claw and tear
Each other's pretty skin and hair !
O jolly husband, have a care !
To-night, to-night, to-night, beware !
We 've brewed a breeze for midnight air,
So full of black-cat squalls and scare,
'T will lay your very eye-balls bare ! "

XVIII.

QUALITY AND QUANTITY.

A WIFE is good ; but too much wife,
Like too much of any thing good,
Say fire, or sweetmeats, or high-seasoned food,
May mar the happiest life.

The rattle and din of tongue-confusion,
Of hard-earned savings the fast diffusion,
The smoke and whiz of family broils,
The smell of liver or tongue when it spoils,
And homemade pickles and peppers, have led
Some cynical men to bless their stars
That they have not been pressed in these wars !
And some have even foolishly said,
Since *one* wife is sometimes *too many*,
'T is better by far no wife to wed,
But go through the world without any.
The fact is, we ought to avoid extremes ;
For instance, Solomon's, who it seems
Had rather too much of wife for his good,
Not to name the enormous amount of food
That such an army of mouths consumed,
And house-rent ; for all must be fed and roomed,
Besides the jams, and jellies, and wines,
For the wives, not to reckon the concubines.
Another extreme is that of St. Paul
Whose rule was, not to marry at all.
St. Paul, we know, was a very good man,
But if the whole race should follow his plan,
The world would soon be in need of no preachers,
Apostles, nor parsons, exhorters, nor teachers,
Nor churches, conventicles, bells nor steeple,
For the reason, the world would soon have no
    people.

And as to the ancient patriarchs ;
Their wives have luckily left behind,
For the use of others, a piece of their mind,
And a few of their most significant marks, —
With feminine forecast very kind, —
In the form of scratches, by teeth and nails,
And scars of tongues, and womanly rails, —
The hieroglyphics, known to fame,
Which all go under the common name
Of ancient hand-guides or finger-marks, —
To bid us beware of the patriarchs
In matters of bigamy,
As the double-headed domestic curse,
And parent of monster progeny.
One wife for a man is not too few,
If she is the wife she ought to be ;
And if she is not, why, two or three,
Or any number you think might do,
Would only make matters worse ;
They 'd only multiply family fights,
And fill up the land with Ishmaelites,
And other tribes whose names end with " tites,"
A regular string of inhuman frights,
And hordes of Arab robbers and beggars,
Besides a host of deserted Hagars.

And therefore every man alive,
In order to have the world to thrive,

Should choose a mate, and marry and wive;
And if in order to keep at bay
Connubial cares, and such, alway,
He tries a bachelor life of revel,
He 'll lead, at least, a doubtful life,
And maybe, in 'scaping the arms of a wife,
Will fall in the arms of the devil.

Though wedlock came from Eden the blest,
A fruitful source of peevish unrest,
However slender her waist may be,
And what other beauties her lord may see,
Is a wife that *can't digest.*
Her hair may curl, and her eyes of blue,
And rosy cheeks, and so on, may do;
And, like the magnet, her heart may be true,
And worthy the best of husband's trust;
And yet, no matter how good and trusty,
She will, if always nibbling a crust,
Be in danger of growing crusty.
'T is all very well that the dear one sings,
And pleasant it is to see a sweet face;
For the head and heart have the highest place;
But liver and lungs are vital things,
And not so exceedingly small;
And no one will wittingly call in question
The fact that the stomach and good digestion
Are the best foundation for all.

Dyspepsia, Proteus of all diseases,
Of all the ages, and every clime,
Will take all their forms, if not each name,
To frighten and shake the dear one's frame,
And threaten her death, from time to time.

Consumption is coming if Susan sneezes,
And phthisic, or asthma, if once she wheezes ;
And liver complaint, from pain in her side,
And hundreds of other complaints beside ;
A chill will cause the dear one to beg you
To run for a cure for fever and ague ;
Unusual pulsations always impart
The symptoms of sudden disease of the heart ;
And gradual swelling and shortness of breath
Mean nothing if not the dropsy, or death.
'T is therefore that healthful body and mind
Are needful in wives of the choicest kind.
That is, if a wife isn't all in your eye,
Choose one who can laugh as well as cry,
Who knows how to romp as well as to sigh,
And to eat and live as well as to die.

And also a man with so much at stake,
For himself, and other folk yet unborn,
Should, both for his own and those others' sake
He hopes to see budding, one by one,
On the fruitful vine, some summer morn,

And bursting out in the light of the sun,
　　Be careful to make
　　No foolish mistake
In taking a wife, lest, haply, he find
He 's chosen one not at all to his mind ;
As hundreds have found by going it blind ;
And instead of a woman of Nature's make,
Find saw-dust and cotton, and paint and dye,
Made artfully up to suit the eye ;
Which he would n't wish to multiply,
If " like makes like " with a progeny.

　　Moreover, he ought to keep himself free
From the old fox-traps, and spring-gun plan,
So not to be caught, as Jacob was ;
(The old folks, you know, were the cause,)
And keep himself, if he possibly can,
From taking the wife of another man ;
Lest after all when married some day,
She give him the slip, and run away,
According to free-love law, set free
By chemical lack of affinity, —
A modern and novel discovery
In matrimonial chemistry.

　　Besides, if he dont get a wife to suit,
He 'll more than likely change to a brute ;
Owing to what is commonly styled,

When both the parties are easily riled,
   An incompatible temper.
The wife of his bosom will snarl and bite ;
And then the fond husband will growl and fight,
   And try to poison, or hemp her,
     For incompatible
     Meaning combatable
   'Twixt opposite parties wed,
Requires the wife, with tongue and scratch,
   And now and then a swoon ;
And the husband, with weapons more than a match,
   To fight from the wane of the honeymoon
   Till one or the other is dead ;
Unless they snap the hymenial tether,
Or sulkily onward, at loggerheads pass,
Like a goring bull and a kicking she-ass
   Unequally yoked together.

The man who married ten thousand a year
Ten children, and widow, felt cheap and flat
When he found the widow was dear at that ;
And he always called her his " *dear* " —
   Meaning herself and her money.
For she was so old, and he was so young,
And she though feeble had *such* a tongue, —
   Not nearly as sweet as honey.
But when she grew old and sickly, fast,
   He almost began to adore her ;

Not knowing, of course, how long she would last,
 Till he came to die before her.

The Knickerbockers did better than this,
 In the olden time of my story :
They thought much more of family bliss
 Than family wealth and glory ;
And found other use for fist and tongue
 Than fighting each other when mated ;
But then the land was *so* very young,
 And *so unsophisticated!*
And man when natural *is so funny,*
And stupidly simple : he slowly learns
That love, and equally silly concerns
Are less important than money.
The Rusticus often excites our pity,
That man should smell so much of green grass,
And burn tallow dips instead of gas,
And learn his breeding in fields, whereas
'T is so much improved in the city !
For Rusticus holds, that Nature provides,
All over the world, and under the sun,
One wife for a man, and only one ;
And that if he take a brace of brides,
No matter how slily the thing be done,
Nor what he may call it by name,
He does a mean act, a sin and shame ;
Because more than one is too many,

And since he has taken more than his share,
Somebody must go without any.

But foul in the country in town is fair ;
As shown by many a Bull and Bear,
Who prowls and paws the city ground,
And gulps his feed from his golden tubs,
And scarcely knows that his calves, or cubs,
Are pasturing all around.
He has a family every one knows ;
His name is on the door where he lives ;
But what are the names of his other wives,
  Nobody knows ;
  Nor where he goes,
When business calls him away, as it does,
Much oftener than it should for his good,
As well as the good of some others.
His children don't know their sisters and brothers,
Though meeting sometimes, and speaking per-
      chance,
In heated saloons, amid the dance,
Or similar place, where they gather ;
And showing still more their ignorance, —
His children dont know their father !

And king Beelzebub kindly consents
To leave his predestined nabob awhile,
Enjoying his nectar, and fortune's smile,

And marble palace, and golden gain ;
Because he likes to have him maintain
A number of such establishments.
   It makes him smile
   To see the guile
By which a man can live in style,
And be so extensive a father!
He winks at the supple knees that cringe
Around the nabob's golden fringe,
His golden showers to gather ;
Like flies and kites that gather to eat
The dainty carcass of tainted meat.
The devil knows what the man is at,
While filling his vessels so :
And as to the tempest, and wrecks, and all that,
There is time for all that below.

AND this is the reason, as far as we know,
Why Saint Brigham Young has such a go,
In Sodom and Gomorrah,
Where Satan's saints, from haunts of sin
Throughout the world, are gathering in ;
And Dead Sea snakes, from crawling round
The globe, at last a den have found,
Where masculine lust, and feminine sorrow,
And all their loathsome litter abound.
The scum of cities sunk for shame,
By floods of fire and sulphurous rain,

In the Old World's lust-polluted plain, —
They meet in the New World's new Salt Lake,
To do Beelzebub's work, the same
As when they flaunted their ancient name ;
And call for another flood of flame
To wipe out the New, as the Old.
Old Satan, of course, makes no complaints,
But smiles, like the sun, on his brazen saints,
Applauding their actions bold ;
And fills their snake-wreathed cups to the brim,
While they bear armsful of fuel for him, —
The dried old lumber, from every clime,
And stubble, long heated in lust and crime,
To make the flame of the coming fire
Burn deeper, and wider, and higher.
He glories to see them riot and revel,
To cure what they call the social evil,
And in the name of the Lord serve the devil,
With Satan's anointing oil and wine ;
And very religiously, in his cause,
Leer both in the face of God and man ;
And sin, undisturbed, on a pious plan ;
Snapping their fingers at human laws,
And laughing at laws divine.
Nor Brigham, chief Saint, asks shades of night
To cover his numerous wives from sight ;
Nor brings up his children in ignorance
Of whom their father may be ;

Like manifold others, begotten of chance,
Afar from the new Dead Sea :
But rather brags of his fatherly power
To call off his offspring, score upon score,
And hear their responses like waves on the shore ;
And fondly hopes for a few dozen more, —
If his vessels come in at the hour.
And Nemesis sleeps on Salt Lake shore,
While Brigham yet counts his harems o'er,
And sees not a cloud to overcast
His glorious future in store.
But if the old devil don't get him at last
Then what is the devil for ?
The butcher, we know, is sure to claim
For slaughter the beasts he owns ;
And Satan with *his* will do the same ;
For he brands them deep, with leprous flame,
That eats to their very bones.
But what is the cause of his long delay,
Till they think the devil is not to pay
For all he has done for his saints,
In spite of grumbling Gentile complaints ?
The reason he does n't torment them now,
As whilom our friend the unhappy Rip,
With witch and nightmare and goblin woe,
Must be, that his spells have bound them so,
He knows they 'll never give him the slip ;
And there 's time for all that below.

But Rip, the unhappy, we 're happy to know
Was afraid of Satan, — was Rip ;
And tried to break from his sulphurous grip,
Before his soul was undone.
Of wives he only wished *one ;*
And honestly thought that one was enough,
And did n't envy the man that had more.
The fact is the witches had been rather rough,
And got to be rather too much of a bore :
They 'd overdone, in their goblin zeal,
By breaking Katrina's spinning wheel,
And whisking away her mother's reel,
And girdling her true-love cherry-tree,
While seeming so sweet on Anneke :
Though Anneke's tongue was far from sweet ;
   And even her temper was sour ;
And all her face grew vinegar-red,
As stamping the floor with her little feet,
   On losing her amiable power,
Her words came down, like hail, on the head
   Of Rip, exposed to the shower.
Nor had she become the least bit thinner,
Although her tongue was so busy a sinner ;
And though the breakfast and supper and dinner
   Were very uncertain things,
Which last would fly away at the hour
   Of meal-time, as if they 'd wings !
The turkeys, the game, and like things good,

Which Rip provided, seemed phantom food ;
And though the larder was full of meat,
Yet half the time he had nothing to eat ;
And that which he had was not over sweet,
When Anneke's temper was sour.

Nor could Katrine, — do what she would,
With gentlest charm, and wisest skill,
And readiest hands to work her will,
And words as soft as softest silk,
Prevent the thunder from spoiling the milk,
Nor witches from spoiling the food !
'T was then that Rip, not always suspicious,
Began, at last, to grow superstitious,
And to link his Anneke with the witches ;
Especially as he found her in niches,
And hide-away places, ghosting about,
At hours when witches were always out.
At any rate, well he knew, 't was she
Who girdled Katrina's cherry tree : —
    For he saw her do it !
    And Anneke knew it ;
And knew that the knife that cut the bark
Of the Homestead-tree, like a thief in the dark,
Cut more than she meant to sever, —
Had clipped the cord, whate'er it might be,
That bound her to Rip forever !

Katrina was patient, and kind, and mild ;
Forgiving, and trusting, as any child ;
    And proved that " silence is golden : "
She nursed, in her heart, the strength of right
By secretly drinking, day and night,
    From well-springs sacred and olden.
And yet she wilted and faded, for all ;
Drooping, as choice and favorite flower
Grows sickly and dies from blighting power
Of some hidden worm, however small.
The warp and woof of her singular doom
Were tangled like those of her husband's loom :
And what could she do but wait, and trust,
As one in such a condition must ?

    And as for poor Rip, why, no one knows,
But a husband, a husband's woes,
    And variegated trouble ;
And Rip was a double husband, which shows
That his, at least, were double.
His farm once flourishing by his skill,
And hardy blows, and sturdy will,
    Was left to Cæsar and weeds,
    And both were going to seeds ;
For nothing can prosper, in field, or town,
If the house we live in be upside down.
The neighbors gave out that Rip was lazy,
Though some, more merciful, called him crazy.

But not a soul but the husband knows
The hidden springs of a husband's woes,
Nor what he drinks from his daily cup ;
For hearts like houses, are sided up,
And roofed, and the curtains hung.
But Anneke had a bell of a tongue,
That must, at all hazards, always be rung ;
And said whatever it had to say,
In a fearless, ringing sort of way ;
So write the chroniclers of that day.
'T is also said that " walls have ears,"
And " a bird will carry away what it hears ; "
And however true, or false this be,
Somebody, if not a bird of the air,
Had borne the news to the Dominie
Of Rip and his partners, foul, or fair,
Which sent the good man to see.

XIX.

WAR.

The Dominie came like a streak of light
On storm-clouds ; happening in while the fight,
In Rip's log-cabin, was at its height ;
Which arose from Katrina's cherry-tree,
Outrageously wounded by Anneke.
And hence it was that it came to pass

The Dominie saw the whole in mass, —
Katrina in tears, the patient Katrine,
Anneke raving and pulling her hair,
And Rip, like a freestone statue, between,
Of motionless, blank despair !
The Dominie ne'er in his life had seen
Such a pandemonium sort of sight ;
Nor a man in such a terrible plight.
He never had seen a man with two wives,
Trying to live two opposite lives,
And honestly striving, with all his might,
To make ends meet 'twixt wrong and right.
Such a war 'gainst Nature day and night,
Poor Rip had waged ; and succumbed in the fight,
As Dominie saw by the flashing light
Of his eyes, and the set of his jaws.
His friend, good Rip, was not what he was :
Nor Anneke, — nor Katrine,
Nor any thing as it had been.
The Dominie gave his hand to Rip : —
Rip crushed it with a spasmodic grip.
His *faith in Dominie had been shaken,*
Like every thing else about Rip :
He 'd found the Oracle was mistaken,
And then had tried Hollands and flip ;
And these having only shaken him worse,
He left the inn, with an inward curse,
And resigned himself to fate.

And fate had made him a shuttlecock,
And bruised him with many a battledoor-knock,
Too horrible to relate.

The Dominie, seeing his woful state,
Spake kindly to him in Dutch ;
But as his ears had been battered dead,
And he did n't hear a syllable said,
It did n't affect him much.
And Anneke's tongue rang out like a bell,
For Anneke had her grievance to tell ;
And Dominie soon had enough to do,
As cook in such a domestic stew !
Nor could he get Anneke's tongue to rest
Till the blushing sun sank down in the west.
And then the Dominie sat awhile,
Rolling his thumbs and trying to smile,
Like an uninvited guest.
But not long sat, in such awkward style,
Before made welcome, by good Katrine,
To gathered up, frugal repast ;
Which she, by leaving the war, unseen,
With womanly tact and kind forecast,
Got ready, with hospitality,
To cheer and freshen the Dominie, —
The Blucher with reinforcements sent
To Waterloo on a smaller scale, —
He looked so jaded and pale.

When this was o'er much time was spent
In talking of life's great mystery,
And strange events ordained to be,
And things we never can understand,
Because our eyes are too dull to see.
When Rip, the silent, suddenly
Arose and seized the Dominie's hand,
And led him forth to an outer shed,
In the loft of which was Cæsar's bed.
Here Rip had seen, though nothing he said,
On many a dark and lone midnight,
Around a dim and sulphurous light,
The shadows of a singular band,
Whose revels had filled his soul with dread.
And here, by pantomimic command,
He bade the astonished Dominie stand ;
And then with trembling hand to his head,
As if to hold his thoughts in his brain,
And rolling his eyes like one insane,
He left the Dominie to remain,
Till mounting the loft and coming again
He bade the Dominie follow.   In vain !
The good man doubted where Rip might lead,
And feared some desperate sort of deed
In Rip's peculiar state.
He did n't like to trust his life
To a man with a double lot of wife,
Alone, at any rate.

But Rip, by an effort, settling his mind,
He followed, at last, not far behind,
Until they both had mounted the loft,
By the aid of a lantern's shielded light;
And there, in the dead of that summer's night,
He saw, in the garret-loft a sight
That made his hair stand up on end
 Through all his life thereafter !
He heard the strangest orgies blend
 With wierd and wildest laughter ;
And heard the good name of Rip, his friend,
 As one who was doomed to slaughter
In that world whence Dives tried to send
 To this for a drop of water.

A group was seated around a table,
On which was a parchment scroll ;
And Dominie, by a feint, was able
To read the names on the roll.
By looking stealthily over the shoulder
Of him who seemed to be chief of the rest,
And much like Buckhout, the innkeeper, dressed,
Though lither, and bolder, and older ;
He caught at a single glance the sight,
Among the names, of the name of Rip,
In letters of bluish brimstone light !
Quick turning, with finger on his lip,
To keep Rip silent, — he held his breath,

And with a face as pale as death,
The Dominie fixed for a fight,
Like virtue arming 'gainst evil :
And then, in the name of good and right,
He grappled with the devil.

A sudden rush, and a flash of flame,
And the battle all was o'er !
For that the Dominie was game
That gang well knew before :
So hustled down, the way they came,
Quick, through a spring trap-door,
And hid themselves, in guilty shame,
In the hay, on the stable-floor ;
For they feared the talismanic name
    Of *good* and *right*,
Which was the Dominie's battle-cry,
When dashing into the fight,
With his sleeves rolled up, to do or die,
In the stable-loft that night.

The fight was o'er, and not a soul
But he and Rip was there ;
And not a speck of the parchment scroll,
That had Rip's name upon its roll ;
And nothing but bed and timbers bare,
And a smell of sulphur in the air !
The lantern was swept away in the fight,

And all was dark, for dark was the night;
But Dominie said, as well he might,
After putting such forces to flight,
That, " *he who earnestly seeks for light*
Will not in the dark be long :.
And he who honestly strives to do right
Will not be left to do wrong."

By this great battle and victory
Rip's confidence in the Dominie
Was fully restored.   Then, arm in arm,
They walked together, in converse free,
The victor without the least alarm,
And Rip with spirits 't was good to see.
The two were like twins, in harmony;
And Castor and Pollux, the Gemini,
Who never fall out, but always agree,
As, arm in arm, they pace through the sky,
Looked down from the starlit canopy,
And smiled to behold them walking there,
So pleasantly, in the midnight air.
And so, in truth, did every star,
Whose eye was able to see so far,
Who happened to be on guard that night,
Express its joy at so goodly a sight,
By shining with more than usual light.
And so did the spirits that dwell in trees,
That tend to their growth, and weave their leaves,

And give them form and color to please,
Who do the most of their work at night;
These seemed to be filled with great delight,
And clapped their hands, and sang a song, —
A many-voiced, dreamy sort of song, —
As if from a vastly numerous throng,
While Rip and the Dominie paced along.

The gossiping chroniclers also say,
That Buckhout stealthily dogged their way,
Like a cowardly wolf who 'd lost his prey;
Leading his roystering tavern-crew,
Smelling of sulphur and looking blue;
And that he boasted, the following day,
Of having played the devil that night
So well that he cheated the Dominie;
As he pretended he 'd often done
Poor Rip, for the sake of a little fun.
But this the chroniclers all agree
Were simply an impossibility;
For the Dominie knew the devil as well
As he did the sound of his own church-bell;
And inn-keepers rather stay home to sell
  Their honest gin,
  In the cozy inn,
With due respect for the author of sin,
Than go to a stable-loft for a revel,
At midnight, merely to *sham* the devil.

At length, their walk and talk being o'er,
They entered again the cabin-door,
To hold a solemn council once more,
Much better prepared than heretofore.

Fair Anneke still remained quite sore;
And hence when the mild-voiced Dominie
Began with a sacred homily
    On the origin of evil,
Descanting with due humility,
If we consider his victory,
    About the devil; —
Saying how great would have been the joy
To earth, on which he had brought the curse,
If he had been held with bolt and bar;
Or chained to the tail of some burning star,
To be dragged for aye round the universe,
As Hector was to Achilles' car,
And dragged three times around Troy; —
Fair Anneke's tongue anon grew worse,
And groaned, and began to make complaint;
And breaking loose from all restraint,
Flashed flaming words from her burning lip:
" She 'd rather be in Beelzebub's grip
Than trampled on as she was by Rip,
A man who was killing himself with flip!
She wished she had her scissors, to clip
The strings of life, to give him the slip!

She wished in her heart she 'd not been born!
And that she had died in the place of Van Horn!
And that she could fly to the top of High Torn,
To live the life of a hermit forlorn,
And never see any more men!"

" Tut, tut!" said Dominie, " hear me out!
You don't know what you 're talking about,
Your wishes are all in vain;
 For born you have been
 In a world of sin,
And can't get out without pain;
And they who play on themselves old Cain,
Murdering their bodies like Abels slain,
To shorten life's road, by cutting 'cross lots,
(Whatever their hope or desire,)
Behave like eels that jump from the pots,
Or frying-pans, into the fire.
And therefore, whatever your ire,
 Or howsoever molested,
Nay, even if trampled on, like a worm,
You 'd better bear it, and wriggle and squirm,
Than leap, like a snap-bug, into the jaw
Of Death; for when you are once in his maw
 You can't get out till digested.
Whereas in this world there is n't a cave,
Or dungeon of sorrow, this side the grave,
You cannot escape from before you die,

If you patiently wait, and fairly try;
For Jonah even got out of the fish.
But you must n't merely whimper and wish,
But go to work, like the son of Kish,
Or a daughter of Shimei.
Which brings me now to the second head," —
Whereat the Dominie looked, in the face,
As if by his subject forcibly led,
(As rigorous needle leads the thread,)
Into a very tight place.
But jogging along, at uneasy pace,
He came to the cross-roads of *Doubly Wed,*
And so on; of which enough has been said.
" And now we want to discover," said he,
" The proper way out, — the remedy.
' *To err,*' (you know the proverb,) ' *is human,*'
Applying of course to man and woman,
To you and yours, to me and to mine;
You know the rest, ' to forgive is divine.'
Now, here was an error without intent,
And the fault is small where none was meant;
For Rip was not the man to consent
A second partner to woo and wed
Without supposing the first one dead.
The same must be true of Anneke.
And hence at this point we all agree
That all the parties are innocent.
But then, in the course of time, 't was seen,

That she who was dead — the good Katrine —
Had come from the regions of death to life.
Of course she was still her husband's wife;
And doubtless it caused her a deal of pain,
On coming to find him married again.

" Well, now, in fatherland we know
Exactly what we 'd have to do :
A man can't have a second wife
During the first one's natural life.
But living here — the country new —
The second knot being duly tied,
When all believed Katrine had died,
I thought that Rip might keep the two,
If wishing, till the thing was tried.
But tried the thing has thoroughly been,
Till all are as tired and cross as sin,
Especially Rip and Anneke.
Besides, the tongues of Rumor are free ;
    The town has an ear that itches ;
And looking around we can't but see
    The work of Satan and witches.
And so I confess, it seems to me
That Rip from Katrine, or Anneke,
    Had better be untied.
The question 's only, which shall it be,
    His first, or second bride ?
A matter of choice entirely free
    Howe'er you may decide.

And now, to make the parting pangs less,
　I 've only a word beside, —
Whoever shall bear this sad distress
　Must not be made a beggar;
Shall not go forth to the wilderness
　An unprovided Hagar;
And as there is n't an Ishmael,
But plenty of water, in spring and well,
And really, as I need not tell,
In this good land no desert at all,
Her hardships, of course, will be but small."

And, then, with wisdom to suit the time,
And a look that was grand to look upon,
The Dominie almost grew sublime,
And seemed like another Solomon.

" Now, ladies ! your choice will simply be
Between the *man* and the *property !*
Your choice is now untrammelled and free ;
The one shall have house and land, in fee,
The other shall merely possess the man ;
That is, if Rip will agree to the plan."

" I do," said Rip, " most cheerfully,
Excepting but the cherry-tree,
Now wounded, with Katrina's name ;
Land or no land, that tree I 'll claim."

Then Dominie turned benignantly
His beaming eyes upon Anneke;
And asked her to freely take her choice.
And Anneke said, " If she had a voice,
At all, in the matter, she 'd take the *farm*.
'T was easy enough," she at once began —
(Her tongue was loose and away it ran) —
" 'T was easy enough to get a *man*,"
(Sarcastic, curling her upper lip,)
" And she did n't feel the least alarm
But that she 'd get a *better than Rip!*
'T was *harder she owned to get a farm*."

Then Dominie asked the fair Katrine
If *she* had a choice what *her* choice would be ?
With blushingest smile that e'er was seen
She modestly answered, " I do agree
To take what is left by Anneke :
My husband is all the world to me."

On which the Dominie bade the three,
For order's sake, and formality,
And that the matter might duly stand,
To arise, and hold each other by hand; —
On either side Anneke and Katrine,
And Rip, the double husband, between.
He then descanted, with solemn air,
On all the events that brought them there,

And wrongs of double connubial lot;
And added, " We now will proceed, with care,
To untie the extra, the second, knot ! "

Addressing himself to Rip and Katrine,
He said, " If you wish and sacredly mean
To hold each other as husband and wife,
In good and evil, through all your life,
And *give to Anneke house and lands*,
Declare it, while holding each other's hands."
They answered, " We do ! " most cheerfully.

Then turning to Rip and Anneke,
He said, " If you still consent and agree,
On terms already mentioned, to be
As if you 'd never been married by me,
Let go your hands, *in sign of release*,
And that you thus part, for life, in peace."

They parted hands ; and Anneke, shorn
Of Rip Van Bigham, was 'gain Van Horn !
She curled her lip, and smiled, and sighed,
As standing apart from Van Bigham's side,
She looked the very *reverse of a bride ;*
While Dominie, with an air of pride,
Pronounced the marriage knot untied ;
Concluding, he hoped they were satisfied.
' For himself he felt he had never done

A wiser action under the sun ;
For Rip and Katrine had ever been one,
Since their marriage morn, in Amsterdam,
Since Death had only played them a sham ;
And Rip had done a noble act,
In making over, by solemn pact,
What Anneke had no right to demand, —
A generous gift of house and land.
And Anneke now was free to choose ;
For soon the yonkers would hear the news,
And he would n't be surprised, at all,
To receive, in a month or two, a call
To make her again a happy bride,
With a knot that need n't to be untied.'
" And, lastly, I trust we 'll all be friends :
Forgive whatever there is to forgive,
Forget whatever is best to forget,
And friendly and lovingly try to live ;
For life has much in store for you yet.
Amen, Amen ; may we all be friends ! "
And thus the strange ceremonial ends.

Then Rip, and Katrine, and the Dominie,
In turn, shook hands with fair Anneke ;
And speaking kind words, in soft Low Dutch,
They seemed to soothe and flatter her much ;
Rip praising her powers and industry,
Especially in matters of food !

And saying, he thought she had tried all she could
While they were living as husband and wife,
To lead him a peaceable, quiet life ;
And how, in his secret heart, he had tried
To regard her as the rib of his side ;
And really thought that he had begun,
Till, finding that Death and the grave had lied,
And had to send back his kidnapped bride,
He knew there could be but only one
For a man to love, as he ought to love :
And matches are made above.

" And matches are also made below ! "—
Said Anneke with her eyes aglow,
And the air of a person who ought to know, —
" Or woman would not be treated so
Outrageously, as all histories show
She always has been since the world began, —
Like a slave, and beast of burden for man.
The girl is a jewel while being wooed, —
A flower, — an angel, — any thing good.
She sings, — oh my ! she sings like a bird !
But as soon as the courting days are over,
And man 's a husband, instead of a lover,
    The flower is crushed !
    Her songs are hushed !
Or, if they are sung, are never heard ;
Her tongue is a bore, if she speaks a word ;

And all her beauty has suddenly fled:
The jewel 's a worthless piece of lead,
The angel is merely a two-legged mule,
To obey the driver, — her husband's rule,
And carry his baggage, and bear the weight
Of any load that his silly pate
May happen to think of, early or late;
And when the poor jade is broken down
He sells her off, to some other clown;
Or turns her out to die, on the town.
Oh the men! the tyrants! the wicked men!
If ever I choose to marry again,
I give the simpleton warning, now,
I 'll teach him what a man ought to know.
And after he takes the marriage vow,
If he don't fulfill it I 'll make him show
The reason why not! a pretty plight
A woman is in if might makes right!
No, sir! I intend to have my way;
I 'll have it all down in black and white;
It 's time a woman had *something* to say!
She 's as good as her master, any day!' "

Rip heard her through, though feeling abused,
And meekly answered, like one long used
To be well pounded, and pestled, and bruised,
    In the matrimonial mortar, —
That what she had said was partly true;

And he desired, as far as he knew,
That every woman should have her due ;
But as to wives — he *could n't stand two.*
He had n't intended to do her wrong,
To crush her flowers, nor hush her song,
Nor hamper, at all, her musical tongue ;
Nor at any time to make her a mule,
And though he 'd acted, he thought, like a fool,
　　He 'd *never intended to court her :*
And *hoped she 'd never forget the fact ;*
And was going on, with more truth than tact,
When, catching a glance of Katrina's eye,
He closed by saying, he hoped she 'd try
To forgive and forget whate'er he 'd done ;
For he felt as sorry as any one,
　　And only meant to confess it ;
She knew he had n't the gift of speech ;
The words he wanted were out of his reach,
　　And so he could n't express it ;
But hoped she 'd only remember the best,
Whatever it was, and forget the rest ;
And wished from his heart she might be blest.

XX.

PEACE.

FAIR Anneke had much more to say ;
But Dominie skillfully hedged the way,
By hinting, that night had turned to day ;
And chronicling cocks were crowing gay ;
And Morning had sent his courier ray ;
And that the usual morning's repast
Was a pleasant way to break one's fast.
He thought the night had been so well spent
That every one ought to be content ;
But *fasting* was *rather a detriment.*

Then Anneke being herself once more,
And Rip and Katrina all their own,
And the reign of the goblins being o'er,
And Order having tripped to her throne,
And every thing to its proper place,
The breakfast came in with easy grace !
  So readily got,
  And smoking hot,
And overflowing with rich supplies,
That Rip in wonder opened his eyes ;
And, when he did so, believed them not,
But sat as if spell-bound to the spot,
  In a dreamy state of delight.

16

And even Anneke looked with surprise,
And uttered sweet words, she hardly knew what,
　Of pleasure, at such at sight.
And all looked on the good Katrine,
As subjects regard a gentle queen,
　Who only thinks of their good ;
And a queen she was ordained to be
Of loving hearts, and a happy home,
Where willing subjects delight to come,
And bow in joyous fealty.
There never had been more savory food,
Nor pleasanter meal, more lavishly praised,
By honester tongues, in happier mood,
In Rip's log-cabin, morn, noon, nor night,
Since the day the cabin was raised.
Which Dominic laid to the timely fight
By which he 'd put the devil to flight,
And so set things in general right.

　　Katrina replied, she knew 't was so ;
" *For evil and wrong bring always woe ;*
But doing right, as far as we know,
Brings joy and peace whatever we do,
And whether our lot be rich, or poor,
The reward of right is ever sure."

　　Then Anneke, soothed by the peaceful meal,
By way of peace-offering dropped a tear,

And a twin-born dove of a sombre smile;
And stated, what all were glad to hear,
That she meant to go, for the public weal,
On a visit *below*, — if Rip, the while,
Would help her on board the *Pioneer.*
Indeed she had thought, for more than a year,
  Of going to Spuyten Duyvil:
She 'd heard so much of that lovely spot,
And wanted to see Hank Lippencott, —
  Her sainted Van Horn's old rival, —
The brother of Brom, the gay-looking man,
Who married last fall the belle of Tappan, —
A schoolmate of hers, whom Rip would remember;
The Dominie married them last November,
A year (the time the cabin was raised)
Or, last of October; — and every one praised
  Brom Lippencott, at the raising.
Well, Hank, his brother, though somewhat crazed,
  Was equally worthy of praising;
For both were good-looking men;
But Hank had been rather sad and forlorn,
Because she jilted him for Van Horn;
And kept *unmarried* since then.
And would n't good Rip take care of the farm,
And keep the crops from suffering harm?
She fancied she 'd better *sell the place;*
Of late, somehow, it had lost its charm,
There had been so much of noise and alarm;

And she felt, in her bones, enough to know
That Spuyten Duyvillers, seeing her face,
Would wish her to stay below;
And as the sloop had been ready to go
For more than a week, with cargo stored,
She thought it better, if Rip thought so,
To pack up at once, and go on board.
And Rip assenting, they all were cheered.
And ere the sun had got very high
That day, on his way to the upper sky,
Fair Anneke bade them all, " Good-by,"
On her way below. And the *Pioneer*
Soon hoisted her sails, with a rousing cheer,
And so the coast was cleared !

XXI.

RECONSTRUCTION.

THE infant day, in the arms of the sun,
   Was shining all aglow ;
The tide had turned, and restless waves
   Began in peace to flow.

The morning blushed to see herself
   Reflected in the bay,
And spreading forth her golden wings,
   Flew round the earth away.

The birds trilled out as sweet a song
  As ear of man e'er heard ;
And Sparkle Creek sang, in the woods,
  As sweet as any bird.

The sunbeams kissed the tears away
  Which earth had shed at night ;
And poplar groves, and forest trees,
  Were laughing with delight.

The bees, rejoicing in their toil,
  And glad that day had come,
Thronged from their city gates in crowds,
  With a city's busy hum.

A hundred bright-winged insect-tribes,
  Happy as day is long,
With bands of music danced for joy,
  And filled the air with song.

The hills were glad, the fields rejoiced,
  Through all the country round ;
And the rustling corn shook golden dust,
  Like manna, on the ground.

The zephyrs wooed the cherry-tree
  That bore Katrina's name,
And amorous sunbeams warmed its roots,
  With new and fruitful flame.

The humble cabin saw it all
  With joy it had not known;
And they that dwelt therein gave thanks,
  As though it were their own.

Within, without, in harmony
  Were all things, great and small;
For the pure in heart love all things pure,
  And Him who made them all.

The stoutest sailors when their ship
  Has lost her reckoning,
And drives before the storm, sing not;
  But safe in port, they sing.

And gentle brooks by sudden showers
  Are choked and cannot sing;
Too full for song, o'erflowing tears
  Are all their offering.

Van Bigham now began to sing,
  Who had not sung before
Since Rip Van Dam so struck him dumb,
  With the heavy news he bore.

His joy-pressed heart flowed not in song
  When lost Katrine, his bride,
Like one new-risen from the dead,
  Stood trembling at his side.

Then came the night whose wrangling storms
　　For weeks obscured the light ;
And birds of song, that sing by day,
　　Sing not in such a night.

But night had passed, — the day had come,
　　Like an angel from above ;
And now all Nature's voices sang,
　　And all their song was love.

Nor was it strange Rip's song should be
　　Of his good wife, Katrine,
For purer love, nor gentler wife,
　　On earth had never been.

His song rang out full many a day,
　　Bright years of joy along,
And truer heart ne'er found a voice
　　In simple, earnest song.

RIP'S SONG OF HIS WIFE.

No happier man can live than I !
　　My dear wife's love is mine ;
And love could not so fill the heart
　　Unless it were divine.

Nor richer man there lives than I !
   Though poor they call my lot ;
For what were all the world to me
   If she should love me not.

One loving heart makes all things bright,
   Like the bright sun in heaven ;
Surely the Lord is very good,
   Or she had not been given.

I envy not the titled great,
   Nor king with jewelled queen ;
For I have home ; and my sweet home
   Is blessed by my Katrine.

No gilded halls, nor palace walls,
   More filled with cheer can be ;
Nor kingdom sweeter to its king
   Than my dear home to me.

What though the rising sun must see
   My busy hands astir ?
The birds are singing while I work,
   And toil is sweet for her.

What though Katrine be simply clad ?
   A queen might wish to wear

The crown of beauty on her brow,
  Than coronet more fair.

And love and truth and gentleness
  Are jewels in her breast;
And surely, with such treasure rare,
  She is not meanly drest.

And all the world doth love Katrine, —
  The very birds come near,
To eat the crumbs she throws to them,
  Without a touch of fear.

I wonder not when she doth come
  They do not fly away,
But gather round the cabin-door,
  To sing for her all day.

Nor that the sunbeams love to pour
  On her their golden shower;
They never kissed a sweeter face,
  Nor loved a purer flower.

The flowers she tends are glad to give
  To her their richest bloom,
And fill the chambers of her heart
  With breath of their perfume.

Their fragrant cells are happy homes
 Of fairy little elves,
Who love to kiss the hands of one
 As gentle as themselves.

Oh happy I with such a wife !
 No joy save that above,
No treasure that the earth can give
 Can equal her dear love.

God keep her well ! let no rude blast,
 Nor cloud of stormy wrath,
E'er touch her gentle form, nor cast
 A shadow on her path !

No word of mine e'er fall on her,
 Which I could wish unsaid,
Should Heaven decree that her pure form
 Must lie before me dead.

But her good words may I so hear,
 And Heaven so hear her prayer,
That when she passes to the sky
 Her steps may lead me there.

ANNEKE SETTLED.

Nor Anneke was less content,
At Spuyten Duyvil, whither went
That whilom widow, — wedding bent,
    That summer day.

She wished to view the lovely spot;
Also her friend, Hank Lippencott,
Van Horn's old rival; and why not?
    It was her way.

Her life with Rip was but a span,
Why should she not, on widow-plan,
Lay siege unto another man,
    With her sweet form?

Hank Lippencott, not iron-clad,
Nor widow-proof, was but too glad
To feel the darts that made him sad,
    And hailed the storm.

The doughty Dutchman, sad though stout,
By Anneke was put to rout,
And yielded e'er a month was out;
    Brave Lippencott!

And hence 't was said, that Anneke
Just glanced at Lippencott, and he
At once sent for the Dominie,
   To tie the knot.

With bridal blush upon her cheek,
She sent to Rip, that very week
To sell her farm on Sparkle Creek ;
   She needed cash.

For she was now the wife of one
Whose love would be to her a sun,
And life with her was just begun !
   This with a dash.

The farm, in time, was duly sold,
And by the vendue turned to gold,
And then to Rip, by neighbors old,
   'T was made to pass.

And Anneke lived many years,
And Lippencott forgot his tears,
When both had fallen, like ripened **pears**,
   Into the grass.

Her numerous daughters, wondrous fair,
Still live, by various names, to bear
Her charms and virtues everywhere,
   And winning heart.

Foremother she of widows young,
Yclept " bewitched," by whose sweet tongue
So many hearts of men are stung,
                    Past healing art ;

And founder of the funeral flames,
Where, unconsoled, they burn their names,
And, phœnix-like, renew love's games,
                    With life's unrest.

Let no one think, in all the land,
He hath the power, with single hand,
Before a child of hers to stand,
                    With unmoved breast.

And till he has, let no one blame
Poor Rip, that, caught by such a flame,
He gave to Anneke his name ;
                    He did his best.

RIP AND KATRINA.

Rip, happy man, and his Katrine
 Lived long, nor loved the less ;
But walked, twin-hearted, all their days,
 The path of pleasantness.

How well they lived 't is good to know,
 With blessings great and small ;
Well known through all the country round,
 And well beloved by all.

The vine beside the cabin-door,
 Shadow of peaceful rest,
Gave fruit hospitable to all,
 And joy to every guest.

Old Cæsar was " himself again,"
 And smiled as he used to smile,
And worked away, as he used to work,
 Singing old tunes the while.

The faithful watch-dog wagged his tail,
 With joy, as heretofore ;
And puss, no longer deemed a witch,
 Lay purring on the floor.

The music of the spinning-wheel
    Joined with Katrine's sweet voice,
And the old, staid rhythm of Rip's heir-loom
    Made the cabin-walls rejoice.

The cherry-tree, though sorely hurt
    By Anneke's jealous knife,
Like the strong love that guarded it,
    Tenacious held to life.

Its wounded form, by nurseful care,
    Soon healed and grew unchecked,
As love survives a thousand shocks,
    Nor dies but by neglect.

Its blushing fruit came, year by year,
    As sure as Summer came ;
And with the signs of Rip's true love
    The tree was all aflame.

And in its branches, every Spring,
    A robin built her nest,
And reared her young, assured that none
    Would harm or dare molest.

The birdlings came, and as they grew,
    The nest still grew apace,

With ample stores to satisfy
  The wants of each new face.

The traveller now, who passes by
  The road where once it stood,
Sees row on row of cherry-trees,
  In all that neighborhood.

These sprang from it. Katrina's tree
  Grew famous in the land,
And spread its loving name and fame
  Afar on every hand.

For when a child was budding forth,
  A tree was planted too,
To be a guardian of its love,
  To God and homestead true.

How long a row Rip and Katrine
  Had planted by their house
We but surmise, but this we know,
  She was a fruitful spouse.

And as their household multiplied,
  The mother's gentle grace
Diffused itself through every heart,
  And shone in every face.

Time, in his car, brought them the gifts
　Which to the good he brings ;
And years, as they went flying by,
　Dropped blessings from their wings.

Their brave young orchards stalwart grew,
　And when the Fall came round
Brought golden apples in their arms,
　And laid them on the ground.

The sweating Harvest stacked her sheaves
　For them, with joyous strains,
And crowded all their garners full
　Of rich and golden grains.

The skillful Summer clothed their fields
　In robes of green and gold ;
And clamorous Winter strove in vain
　To pinch their guarded fold.

From their most bounteous house, so blessed
　In basket and in store,
No needy suppliant shivering passed,
　Nor hungry from the door.

Their flocks brought forth abundantly,
　And fields were multiplied,

17

Until their humble farm stretched forth
　　Its acres, far and wide.

Led by his gentle wife, good Rip
　　Rejoiced, with her, to stand
By holy altar, and became
　　The Dominie's right-hand.

Their children followed in their steps,
　　And sang the songs divine ;
And ate and drank, in the holy place,
　　The sacred bread and wine.

Their children's children follow them,
　　In this good land of ours ;
As in the pathway of the sun
　　Walk fruitful fields and flowers.

The land is blessed by such as they,
　　And by their honest blood,
And stalwart limbs, holds on her way
　　For liberty and God.

For God and freedom well they fought,
　　In stormy days of yore,
When the infant land was borne aloft
　　In the iron arms of War.

And when the lion sprang upon
    The stripling in his path,
Again their trusty swords they drew,
    And smote him in their wrath.

And when the fiery traitor-snake
    Rattled for deadly strife,
They sprang upon his crested head,
    And saved their country's life.

From every hill and glen along
    Brave Hudson's glorious banks,
They, like the river's sweeping waves,
    Poured their resistless ranks.

They sprang to arms, not moved by fame,
    But patriot's glowing sense,
That fused their souls, and made their hearts
    A shield for her defense.

And on the land, on sea and lake,
    In battles fierce and bold,
They showed the souls of fathers brave,
    And blood of vikings old.

In leaden hail and thunder crash,
    When brave men held their breath,

Theirs were the hearts that would not yield
    To any foe but death.

How well they fought, how long they fought,
    The rolls of honor show ;
And when they fell they always fell
    With faces to the foe.

Nor yet alone on bloody seas,
    Nor on the battle-field,
These children of the brave and good,
    Their loyal service yield.

No homes of theirs have treason hatched,
    To strike, with bloody hand,
The mother dear that nourished them,
    And slay their native land.

Nor skeptic bands from them have stalked,
    To curse the ground they trod,
With treason flaunting on their flag,
    Against their fathers' God.

With watchful prayer, and sleepless eye,
    They guard their country's gates ;
And, heart to heart, they form the chain
    That binds in one her States.

Their sturdy arms her forests fell,
 They cleave her virgin soil ;
And from the earth her treasure bring,
 And build her State with toil.

Their daring keels plough every sea.
 And from all climes they meet
With gathered wealth and jewels rare,
 To cast them at her feet.

And she, amid her untold wealth,
 And crowned with jewels stands ;
But counts, by far her richest gems,
 Their loving hearts and hands.

For truer hearts and firmer hands
 The world hath never seen
Than those bequeathed to our dear land
 By Rip and his Katrine.

XXII.

MORAL.

To all who dwell on Tappan Zee,
 Or any sea beside,
I would this truthful tale might be
 A compass, chart, and guide.

Let not a parson shrink from duty,
   Whate'er his duty be,
Because of wife, or wealth, or beauty,
   Or best of tongue, or tea.

Let not a widow haste to wed
   A man bereaved by death,
Nor think his first wife surely dead
   Because she's out of breath.

Nor widowers hurry, when forlorn,
   That other wives be found
Before they're sure that those they mourn
   Are cold and under ground.

And let all men be sure of this, —
   That for the happiest life
Enough's enough of any bliss,
   Especially of wife.

THE END.

HYMN.

BY REV. EDWARD HOPPER, D. D.

For watch and ward through FIFTY years,
    O'er storm-tossed brothers of the sea,
And gathered fruits of toil and tears.
    Glad thanks we bring. O God ! to Thee.

We heard Thy voice. "The sea is mine."
    And followed where Thy footsteps led :
While from Thy presence light divine
    A glory on our pathway shed.

The waves grew calm beneath Thy feet:
    Wild spirits hushed their stormy breath:
And from the depths came pæans sweet
    From rescued souls redeemed from death.

On every sea, to every shore
    Sail Thou, O Christ ! Stretch forth Thy hand
Till storms shall sweep the waves no more,
    Till death no more shall sweep the land :

Till all the lands their jewels bright
    Bring forth to deck Thy brow alone :
And every ocean, robed in light,
    Reflects the glory of Thy throne !